HOW TO START AND RUN A

B&B

IN

FRANCE

HOW TO START AND RUN A

B&B

— IN —

FRANCE

· REVISED AND UPDATED · SECOND EDITION · 2ND

DEBORAH HUNT

howtobooks

Published by How To Books Ltd,
Spring Hill House, Spring Hill Road, Begbroke,
Oxford OX5 1RX, United Kingdom.
Tel: (01865) 375794. Fax: (01865) 373162.
email: info@howtobooks.co.uk
www.howtobooks.co.uk

First published 2003
Reprinted 2004
Second edition 2008

Line drawings by Deborah Hunt

British Library Cataloguing in Publication Data
A catalogue record for this book is available from
the British Library

ISBN: 978 1 84528 272 1

Cover design by Baseline Arts Ltd, Oxford
Produced for How To Books by Deer Park Productions, Tavistock
Typeset by TW Typesetting, Plymouth, Devon
Printed and bound by Cromwell Press Ltd, Trowbridge, Wiltshire

NOTE: The material contained in this book is set out in good faith for general guidance
and no liability can be accepted for loss or expense incurred as a result of relying in
particular circumstances on statements made in the book. Laws and regulations are
complex and liable to change, and readers should check the current position with the
relevant authorities before making personal arrangements.

Contents

Note from the Author   xi

1   Before You Begin   1

Living the Dream   2
What is a Bed & Breakfast?   3
Qualifications   4
The Rewards   5
One or Two Bedrooms   5
Three or Four Bedrooms   6
Five or Six Bedrooms   7
Who Runs a B&B?   8
A Balanced Business   9
Planning the Move   9
Tips   10

2   Choosing the Property   12

Cost   12
The Quick Way In   12
Start a New Business   15
In a Village   16
Near a Main Road   16
Sea, Country, Mountain   17
Near a Tourist Attraction   18
Towns   18
Where to Avoid   19
The House   20
The Land   21
Tips   22

3   Buying Your Property   23

People you are Likely to Meet   23
A Different System   23
Estate Agent   24
Making an Offer   24
Surveyor   25
Architect   26

Notary		26
Preliminary Contract		27
Land Registry Plan		28
Fixtures and Fittings		28
Completion		29
Taking Possession		29
Tips		29

4 Renovating Your Property | | **31**
The People you will Meet		31
House in Good Condition		31
Old Houses Needing Restoration		32
Notification of Minor Work		35
Preliminary Planning Permission		35
Planning Permission		36
Building Regulations		36
Using an Architect		37
Large Building Projects		37
Minor Building Projects		39
Building-it-Yourself		40
The Building Work		41
Tips		49

5 Designing the Interior | | **50**
Ambience		50
Style		51
How to Acquire the Furniture		52
Bedrooms		53
Bathrooms		57
Kitchen		61
Dining Room		62
Lounge		64
Games Room		66
Hall		66
Guests' Kitchen		67
Storage		67
Utility Room		68
Office		68
Staff Quarters		68
Tips		69

6   Barns and Outside   **70**

Small Outbuildings   70
Large Barns   71
Parking   72
Garden   72
Terrace   73
Swimming Pool   73
Grow Your Own   78
Animals   78
Boules Court   79
Children's Area   79
Other Leisure Activities   79
Woodland and Hedges   80
Yet More Land   80
Extra Accomodation   81
Septic Tank   81
Rubbish   81
Tips   82

7   The Table   **83**

Breakfast   83
Table d'Hôte   86
Profit   87
Lighten the Load   88
Demi-pension   89
Children   89
The Hosts   89
Lunch   90
Regional Cooking   91
Dinner   92
Some Further Points   96
Diets   96
Barbecue   97
Gourmet Dinner   97
Christmas and New Year   98
Supplies   99
Frozen Food   99
Reservation   99
The Chef   100
Tea   100
Tips   101

8 Finance and Administration   **102**

Finance   102
Early Difficulties   103
Grants   103
Prices   104
Filling the Rooms   106
Booking   107
Cancellations   110
Paying   110
Telephone   111
Computer   112
Snail Mail   113
Insurance   113
Accountant   115
Tips   116

9 Keep it Clean   **117**

Cleaning   117
Maintenance   118
Linen   118
Curtains   121
Laundry   122
Equipment and Materials   122
The Kitchen   123
Smoking   124
The Wildlife   124
The Welcome   126
Tips   126

10 Dealing with Officialdom   **127**

Chamber of Commerce   128
Self-employed   129
Limited Company   129
Providing Identity   129
Bank Account   130
Rates 1   130
Rates 2   131
Rates 3   131
Income Tax   131
VAT   132

Health Care   132
Pension and Allowances   134
Social Security   135
Drinks Licence   135
Motor Vehicles   136
TV Licence   136
The Police   136
Fire and Ambulance   137
Electricity, Gas and Water   137
The Black   138
Where to Get Help in France   138
Tips   139

11 Not a B&B   140
Farming   140
Viticulture   141
Gîtes   142
Activity Holidays   143
Other Possibilities   144
Not a *Chambres d'Hôtes*   146
Tips   146

12 Organising the Publicity   148
The Organisations   149
The Web   153
Bed & Breakfast Guides   154
Magazines, Newspapers, Directories   158
Photographs   159
Brochure and Stationery   160
Outdoor Signs   162
Exploit other Possibilities   163
Repeat Business and Recommendations   163
Business Name   164
Chèques Vacances   165
The First Year   165
Tips   166

13 Looking After the Staff   167
Yourselves   167
Relatives and Friends   169

Children   169
Help in the House   169
Specialist and Gardening Help   171
Doing Business with the French   172
Keeping up the Standard   173
Managing your Time   173
The Long Winter Months   174
The Proprietors   174
Tips   185

14   Keeping the Customers Happy   186
Nationality   186
Age   187
Holidays   187
Other Reasons for Coming   188
When do they Come?   189
The Welcome   190
Etiquette   191
Children   193
Disabled and Elderly Customers   194
Customers' Animals   195
Customers you could Do Without   195
Tourist Information   196
Strangers in a Foreign Land   197
The Final Analysis   197
The End of the Day   198
Tips   199

Postscript   200

Appendix A – Useful Books   201

Appendix B – Useful Addresses   205

Index   208

Note from the Author

The tourist business moves fast, so those who don't keep up to date will find that customers soon go elsewhere. Many things have changed since this book was published in 2003, hence the need for a revised edition.

The big changes are:

- The arrival of the internet – in 2003 it was very new but now it's a major factor, so I have incorporated the many resulting changes in methods of communicating and advertising.

- The tourist market becomes ever more global as the price of air fares relative to earnings reduces, so B&B proprietors must put more effort into publicity to capture their share.

- Standards go up all the time, so don't be left behind.

- In 2003, when the first edition of this appeared, the euro had only arrived the year before and we in France were still struggling with this funny money. Now we have come to know the best and the worst of it. The best is that France is making a determined effort to hold its premier place in the world of tourism. The worst is that we've had a dose of inflation and cheap properties for conversion into B&Bs have totally disappeared.

- Bureaucracy marches on in spite of a new government pledged to reduce it, so the book has been updated accordingly.

As well as the necessary revisions, each chapter includes new ideas for running your business. So here's wishing you a plentiful supply of satisfied customers and a reasonable profit for all the work.

Deborah Hunt

Dedication

This book is dedicated to my grand-daughter,
Francesca Viviana Teresa

1

Before You Begin

Living in France has the following advantages for the British:

- The cuisine and lifestyle are highly regarded.
- It is our nearest foreign country.
- It is in the European Union.
- Property is cheaper.
- Best health service in the world.
- Less people per hectare and less vehicles per kilometre.
- Better climate (mostly).
- Many of us have already spent holidays there.

And disadvantages:

- Separation from family and friends.
- Life as an ex-pat can be difficult and frustrating at first.

- They speak French.
- Driving is a competitive sport.
- Baked beans/Cheddar cheese/Marmite are hard to find.

So much for living there. How about living there and running a B&B? Advantages:

- No work permit needed (for EU residents).
- More tourist visitors than any other country in the world.

And disadvantages:

- *Taxe d'Habitation, Taxe Foncière, Taxe Professionelle, Taxe sur le Valeur Ajouté, Contributions Sociales, Assurance Vieillesse, Mutuelle, Impôt sur le Revenu.* (Each will be explained in Chapter 10.)

We found that the French were very reticent about giving out information. That is the opposite of the USA where they shower you with stuff. A French person explained that they think it impolite to give gratuitous information because it implies ignorance on the part of the listener. Of course they will always answer a direct question, but that supposes you know what questions to ask. So I shall be trying to forestall as many questions as possible.

LIVING THE DREAM

By now you will have made up your mind about living in France. Moving to another country after a career in the UK has become so popular it has even acquired the name 'living the dream'. You come for the laid-back lifestyle in a better climate, the cheaper property, and to get away from the stress of the 12-hour a day job with suits, meetings and sales targets. Unfortunately, some people have to earn a living. The most popular choice for foreigners is the leisure industry because a formal training isn't essential. However, you have got to cope with a new country, a new language and a new job, all at once; and it can be daunting.

If the choice is to run a Bed & Breakfast I will help you to:

◆ Choose the property.
◆ Adapt or restore it.
◆ Make the business profitable.
◆ Avoid the pitfalls.
◆ Cope with the formalities.
◆ Advertise effectively.
◆ Make your guests recommend you and come back again.

WHAT IS A BED & BREAKFAST?

The word 'hotel' is universal, but there are many names for staying as a paying guest in a private house or very small establishment. In English-speaking countries, it's 'bed and breakfast' or 'guest house' or 'inn'. In French-speaking countries, it's *chambres d'hôtes*. Not only does the name differ, but the concept does too. Since so much of French life revolves around the table, it's not surprising to find that many such establishments serve meals, and it is the only country with a name for this presentation, which is *table d'hôte*.

The well known formula of B&B was pioneered in Britain over 100 years ago, originally mostly in seaside resorts. France doesn't have this tradition. For inexpensive lodgings there were only *pensions* or the cheaper hotels. *Pensions* were more than a B&B because they always served meals, but less than a hotel with its restaurant service, and they were always in noisy town centres. With their antiquated plumbing and rock-hard bolsters, they have gone now. In 1954, the organisation *Gîtes de France* was jointly founded by the ministries of tourism and agriculture to promote the use of farm dwellings as holiday *gîtes* because rural areas were losing their populations. This provided extra income to farmers and a boost to tourism. It was, in fact, a winner all round and the word *gîte* has subsequently entered the English language. In 1969 they also added the bed and breakfast concept to this established brand with a well-known logo. However, while the idea has taken off the term *chambre d'hôte* has not had the same success and the words 'bed & breakfast' are frequently used in France. A *chambres d'hôtes* can be as small as one bedroom and serving only breakfast, up to a *château* with every luxury and serving gourmet meals. The maximum number of guests is fifteen in five bedrooms, though some *départements* will allow a sixth if it is for the disabled. However, six bedrooms requires the premises to be classed as a hotel and subject to onerous planning, health and fire regulations which, mercifully, are much lighter for a B&B. Meals can only be served to resident guests. In the UK, the smaller of these establishments would be called a 'B&B', and the larger a 'guest house'.

The B&B concept has increased enormously in the past few years; some departments have seen the number triple in the past decade. Fortunately, there are many more customers, both because we take more trips and because the big chain hotels become ever more bland. They have spread from small beginnings in the country to appearing in towns. *Gîtes de France* has stayed with its country roots, but there are other organisations to join; membership is entirely optional – see Chapter 12 for details. Most grade their members in some way, however hotel stars are not used. The *Gîtes de France* grades of one to four *épis* (ears of corn) are the most widely known grades and are used in this book.

QUALIFICATIONS

Although English is the international language of tourism (aren't we lucky?) if you're going to live in France you have **got** to learn French and should start **now**. You should try to start going to classes before leaving the UK and you'll push yourself more if these lead to an exam; alternatively, enrol yourself on a total immersion course. Choose one that is professionally set up, not a holiday masquerading as lessons. Remember, it will be cheaper if you can attend as a day student. See 'Useful Addresses' or contact your local authority for what is available near you. For those whose O- and A-level French were a long time ago, it is a matter of recapturing that standard, and classes will be better than doing it alone. I'm not saying you have to be fluent, but you need to be able to cope with a wide variety of situations. My one caveat on language courses is: if you plan to do dinners, should one of you go to a short professional cookery course?

THE REWARDS

You'll be working seven days a week in July and August, and long days at that if you do dinners. The 35-hour week does not apply to the self-employed. However, there is no travelling, and for most of the rest of the year you can work at your own pace. Even though you may drive yourself hard, it is still less stressful than working for someone else. It has to be said that you don't make much money in the first few years, possibly even a loss at first. But by the third or fourth year the business should be established and you should be making some profit. Providing, that is, you haven't taken on too much, have chosen the property carefully, and kept a tight control of the expenses.

ONE OR TWO BEDROOMS

The income will be small, so you must be doing it to supplement another source. Really it can hardly fail to pay **provided** you don't spend too much on improvements or advertising. It will pay because otherwise the rooms will presumably just be standing empty except when there are friends or relatives visiting. When it's paying guests the extra expenses will hardly be noticed.

Improvements

After adding a bathroom to each bedroom, **do not** spend too much. Since the bathrooms will increase the value of the house, you don't need to attribute all the cost to the miniature B&B business. Though if it proves exceptionally expensive to add two bathrooms, and the rooms have to share, this may be the best option. In this case both rooms can only be let to one family at a time. The paying guests **should not** share a bathroom with the hosts. In a two-storey house you could devote the first floor to the guests, and if it's empty in the winter there's no need for heating. It **will not** pay to put a swimming pool in just for the visitors; but if you want one anyway, here is a wonderful chance to help pay for it.

Dinner

If you offer dinners at all, you could make it only once a week – say on arrival or Saturdays. You want to get to know people if they are staying *en famille*, as the French would say, but it would be very onerous to do it every night.

Advantages
- Low capital expenditure.
- Easy to discontinue the business.
- Can pick and choose the guests.
- Bedrooms available for own family and friends when required.
- Avoids the loneliness of living in an isolated property.

Disadvantages
- Low income.
- Loss of privacy.

THREE OR FOUR BEDROOMS

This number of rooms gives a great variety of establishments:

1. It could be a reasonable business in its own right.

2. It could be part of the development plan for something larger.

3. If some of the bedrooms are a suite of two rooms then it does form a larger enterprise and could hold 10–12 guests.

The *chambres d'hôtes* organisations class a suite as one room, and it is a very useful arrangement. A children's room can be entered via the main bedroom (and locked when not in use), or it could be a mezzanine, and both share the bathroom. Three or four bedrooms will not produce a living but will be a substantial addition to another income.

Improvements
I assume you have a house with at least four or five bedrooms and two or three reception rooms. I trust the house and services are in reasonable condition, because the scale of the business will not pay for a major restoration. Maybe you wanted to restore the property anyway and are only looking to the B&B to help out. Otherwise, as before, adding extra bathrooms is the major expense.

Dinner
This can depend on how much you like cooking because it will not be on a scale to make a big difference to the income. If there are restaurants nearby it's optional, but if you are isolated then it's essential.

Advantages

◆ Moderate capital expenditure.
◆ Can be run by one person, or a retired couple.
◆ Doesn't need too large a house.
◆ Justifies some cleaning help.

Disadvantages

◆ Does not produce enough income for a couple to live on.
◆ Loss of privacy.
◆ Needs to be well advertised, but cost not always justified by results.

FIVE OR SIX BEDROOMS

This is a serious business and to make a success of it you will need real business acumen. To make a reasonable living for two people, you will need one or more of the following:

1. *Table d'hôte.*
2. Open all year in a location where this will be effective.
3. Have some other activity such as self catering *gîtes*, or classes or a sport.

It will be a full time occupation and will need some paid help if there are only two of you and you do dinners. If more than two partners you will have to promote the business really extensively.

Advantages

◆ Can produce a good income.
◆ Justifies cleaning, or catering, or gardening help.
◆ Justifies the privacy of own separate accommodation.
◆ Good use for a large property.
◆ Great job satisfaction in having created a viable business.

Disadvantages

◆ Large capital expenditure.
◆ Long hours, seven days a week in high season.
◆ Dinner for more than ten every day difficult without experience.

- Six bedrooms incurs the expense of fire regulations.
- If you have a large garden with a pool and you offer a complete holiday experience with full board, then a couple **cannot** manage this on their own.

WHO RUNS A B&B?

Normally it is a couple or other family group. I assume you know each other well enough to assess whether you will make a good team. Setting up in business with friends is a different matter. Do be very cautious because there is a saying that it is easier to get divorced than to break a business partnership. At the very least take a holiday together to see if you get on. Before you even begin, make a formal agreement on the terms for breaking up. How many partners are there going to be in this enterprise? If it is more than two, then even a large B&B on its own is unlikely to produce enough income.

Since the cost of property and buying an existing business or setting up a new one is much less in France, it tempts people who would find a similar enterprise in the UK totally out of their reach. This makes it attractive for younger people, but they still need a steady income for many years yet. Either they must work very hard at the B&B business or must have another income.

For those at or near retirement age I must ask: how old are you? Sorry for such an impertinent question. Just letting a spare bedroom or two will be quite feasible into your eighties provided you can manage the stairs. But a serious business requires such a big capital investment that it really needs a ten-year run to get a return. Possibly you have taken early retirement, in which case project forward to see if you think you will still be fit enough or have the energy for the work. Older people do have one advantage: their pensions will soon arrive or perhaps already have. This will smooth over any rough patches.

Paradoxically running a B&B is ideal for shy people. You meet many guests you would be far too timid to approach socially.

A BALANCED BUSINESS

The most common cause of failure is taking on too much: too big a house or too grandiose a scheme. The French are amazed at the scale of some of the crazy ideas these foreigners have. They are grateful of course for the amount of money we lavish on some of their ruins. In fact do not do in France something you would not dream of doing at home. Be prudent, do not borrow too much, and always reckon that whatever you are doing will overspend. Budget that there will be no profit at all at first if you are doing building work and precious little in the early years if you are starting the business from scratch. It will take three to five years to build the business up and even then there can be bad years through no fault of your own. There are national and international events that seriously damage the tourist trade, or disaster can strike you personally. So always keep a reserve.

Starting right in with the maximum number of bedrooms intended is the truly commercial way. You build the business up quickly and get a proper return on the money spent as soon as possible. It is a great incentive to **have** to fill all those rooms. But if you lack experience, are short of funds, or are nervous about putting so much money into the venture; then you may prefer to proceed cautiously. You could start with two bedrooms, and add further facilities and another bedroom each year. In this case you **must** set a limit, say five years, by which to have finished the improvements and not spend any more. If you keep on dabbling right up to the time you give up or sell, you won't have had a full return on the investment.

PLANNING THE MOVE

It is not the French way to buy and sell property on the same day, though it can be done. Nor would I like to be involved in the complexities of selling in one country and buying in another on the same day. Unless you have the capital, it is best to sell in the UK first. You then know exactly how much you have made, and, with it earning interest, you can afford to rent until you are established in France. The furniture can be stored with a firm that does international removals, and you can take your time for a thorough house search.

Possibly you are considering keeping your former home and letting it, or buying a smaller one as a pad. Realistically I do not think you will have the time, and you will lose bookings by being absent from the B&B for long periods. Also, whichever house you are not in needs looking after. It is much better to sell the UK house **before** the final search in France, so that you are a cash buyer and can negotiate from a strong position.

The property search can begin before you go to France:

1. Search the internet.
2. Go to a French property exhibition.
3. Read the 'French Property News'.

For details of the last two see under 'French Property News' in 'Addresses'. Then, for a serious search, the best way is to hire a *gîte* for a month or more in the winter. Find names in the holiday brochures and see what offers you can get for a long winter let, not forgetting to check that there is central heating. If the owners are British and resident on site, so much the better, as they will be a fund of local knowledge and can give tips on buying in France arising from their own recent experience.

Don't despair if you can't find anything suitable at a price you can afford. There are ways and means. Here's one idea, but only for the expert DIYer or builder. Buy something small and needing renovation in your chosen area. Live in it while one person goes out to work and the other renovates it, then after a year search for what you really want and sell the first one.

You must also engage in some industrial espionage, by which I mean staying the night in at least six other B&Bs. You will learn a lot and begin to form your own opinions about how to run your own place. It will give a great feeling of superiority because of course you will also decide to do it better.

TIPS TO MAKE IT PAY

- ◆ Decide on the size of the business and do not take on too much.
- ◆ Do plenty of preliminary research.
- ◆ Be absolutely sure all the partners form a good team.

TIP FOR LEARNING FRENCH

◆ Classes with a formal exam produce the best result.

2

Choosing the Property

COST

A house with four or more bedrooms, in reasonable condition and with some land, will cost at least €500,000; this will be less in remote areas, more in towns and nearly full English prices in Paris and Provence. House prices increased by 86 per cent between 1998 and 2004, but seem to be stabilising now. Nothing like that has ever happened before and naturally the French blame foreigners, but the same has happened all over Europe. That still leaves property much cheaper than in the UK. For your money you'll get much more land but I'm afraid houses generally are not maintained to our same high standards. Very cheap, unrestored wrecks have almost disappeared from the market.

THE QUICK WAY IN

Have you thought of buying a B&B as a going concern? Here are the advantages:

1. You can move in, take two weeks to settle down, and start making money in week three.

2. All costs are known in advance.

3. There should be plenty of advice from the previous owners.

4. You can probably buy the contents (furniture, curtains, linen, tableware) very reasonably.

5. It can take five years to build up a business; you are coming into one already established.

6. You get the benefit of all the advertising in previous years.

7. You can examine the previous year's accounts.

Here are the disadvantages:

1. The building may not be as sound as it looks and the DIY may be badly done.

2. The services may be poor.

3. You are taking on the reputation of the previous owners.

4. You are stuck with the previous owners' taste.

5. Due to limited supply, there will be little choice of region.

6. You may want to run it differently, so there will be little benefit from buying a going concern.

Think about it seriously. I see the main advantage being that you can start earning straight away. If you have **got** to earn a living this is important. But you would have to make sure the previous owners had taken firm advance bookings, that the clients have all been informed of the change of ownership, and if a deposit has been paid you would have to keep to the same prices. If you've not bought the furniture it will be best to close for the winter because there will be a lot of re-decorating – even removing pictures leaves a mark. And there are bound to be other maintenance items that need attention.

The dream of converting an old property which you have bought cheaply is seductive, but it can take years for the building work, and more years to build up the business. While it is important to look at the last year's accounts, they may not tell you much. Some people about to sell have let the place run down, particularly if the owners are getting divorced or there is some other family problem. The place may be looking a bit tired or there may be scope for increasing the prices and for advertising more effectively. Have an accountant look at the figures. He'll need to be bilingual if they are in French. He must then advise whether the business could make a living, taking into account any mortgage and the projected income.

Any goodwill element can be expected to be included in the asking price, but check this. If the owner will not come below the asking price, you may be able to negotiate to include the furniture. But check that it's worth having. With several bedrooms, the value of the second-hand contents is about £10,000 or more depending on quality. It would cost a lot more than this to buy it all new. Make quite sure you have a detailed inventory.

You should be able to pick up most of the business that the previous owners were generating. Don't close for too long, and don't let the business die away even if you are planning to make changes later on.

A lack of French may be the biggest hurdle in taking over a going concern. It would be slightly easier to start in the winter with less customers around. You would certainly have severe difficulties with several bedrooms and starting in high season, unless you have hotel experience. Regrettably some business does drop away when new proprietors take over. Many previously faithful clients will not come again to new owners, especially if of a different nationality, and the locals will not come until they've had time to size you up. Advertising should be discussed with the vendors early on to see if they will help in getting your's underway, otherwise it will be very late in the day if you wait until you take possession.

START A NEW BUSINESS

Location

'Almost no single mistake is fatal' (so says Bill Gates of Microsoft fame, when he lectured on running a business). I'm afraid that choosing the wrong building in the wrong location could well be such a mistake. First of all, you need to be located where people want to go and the top favourites for the significant nationalities are:

French	Seaside/*La France Profonde* (very rural France)/large towns on business/everywhere for visiting relatives/skiing
British	Provence thanks to Peter Mayle/the Dordogne by which they also mean the Lot/skiing
Americans	Historical sites e.g. Chartres, Avignon, the Loire Valley, Bayeux where they can take in Omaha Beach
Belgians	SW, especially Quercy (old name for Lot and Tarn & Garonne)
Dutch	Unpopulated areas such as Compiègne that can easily be reached for a weekend break, otherwise they will be camping
Germans	Provence/Riviera
Spanish	Don't travel much, but do like the theme park Futurama at Poitiers
Swedish	Prefer to have English hosts as they generally find the French language difficult
Italians	The Alps for skiing
Japanese	Travel in large groups so B&Bs not suitable

And **everyone** loves Paris.

These are, of course, stereotypes and experienced travellers will be found anywhere in small numbers, but naturally the more popular the area the more competition there will be. If you have a link to any nationality can you exploit this and locate yourself where your compatriots like to go?

So much for potential guests. How about yourselves? Could you cope with the isolation of truly rural living? Or if one of you needs to work, should you be near a large town? There's little employment to be found in the countryside, that's why many of the young people have left and property is cheap. And what about the children? If they're used to city life with all its out-of-school activities, they may well complain there's **nothing** to do in the country.

IN A VILLAGE

In my opinion B&Bs are too few in some of the most picturesque villages in the world. There are many advantages. You don't have to provide dinners as there will be restaurants nearby. You will be near a baker for the fresh bread and croissants, and near most of the other support services you need. There will be only a small garden if any at all. In fact a very manageable business. However, the downside is the lack of parking. Maybe you can find something not too far away.

There are 152 villages classified by the government as '*Les Plus Beaux Villages de France*'. No chain hotels here with their neon signs, but very suitable for a B&B if you don't mind being told exactly what you can do with the exterior of your property. There are even a few without a single *chambres d'hôtes*. Go to www.villagesdefrance.free.fr for the list of villages. But there are many more delightful villages not quite in the first rank.

NEAR A MAIN ROAD

Of course you can't advertise on an *autoroute* (motorway), but your brochure could stress that you are not far from a junction. This works better in the north for all those Europeans making the long journey south.

Not everyone rushes along motorways. The *Routes Nationales* ('A' roads) still carry plenty of traffic and you can have a sign actually on the roadside.

Have you heard of the '*bis*' roads? You are a real Francophile if you know that '*bis*' is short for *bison futé* (literally: cunning buffalo). They are government designated alternatives to the main roads and are for drivers who want to enjoy the scenery. Just the people you are after. There is a free map available at motorway service areas and some garages and tourist offices.

You need to be far enough from the road for noise not to be a problem, but not so far that people get lost. You really should do dinners as travellers don't want to go out again. The clientele will be all one night stays, and the nearer the channel ports or tunnel you are, the longer the season will be.

SEA, COUNTRY, MOUNTAIN

See Chapter 8 for figures on the big difference in occupancy rates between a country location and a village centre. Don't kid yourself that you will be able to fill all the rooms for most of the year in a remote area.

These scenic locations are for the longer stay holiday, though you'll still get a few single-night customers. You'll have to offer dinners and give some thought to what clients are going to do for lunches even if you don't provide them yourself.

At the sea you'll want to make a big pitch for children. If you've said 'near' the sea, don't be too far away – no one likes that. There is no need to provide much in the way of facilities unless you wish.

The French have a deep attachment to their countryside and a working farm is very popular, so you will want to join Accueil Paysan (see Chapter 12 on publicity). Other nationalities too love an old farmhouse in the country. If it's not a working farm and not by the sea, and you want long stay visitors, then you really should have a swimming pool and try to provide as many other activities as possible. There may be very little in the vicinity.

In the mountains there may be skiing which gives a winter season. And you'll get a summer season too, especially individualists who appreciate the scenery, the air and the tranquillity. I saw one B&B in such a location that advertised 'no TV, no radio, no traffic'. Quite so.

The main disadvantage of most of these situations is the short season. There is a big capital investment all for four months of the year, and even then you are not likely to be full in June and September. If there's a sporting activity you're keen on yourself, perhaps you could incorporate it in your holiday promotion: sailing, canoeing, riding and fishing come to mind. There is an extensive network of *grandes randonnées* (hiking trails) and although some hikers consider B&Bs too frilly you might catch some if you are well placed.

NEAR A TOURIST ATTRACTION

France has more world class historic sites classified by UNESCO than any other country (*see Fig. 1*). Most are in towns but you don't have to be right alongside to list it as a local attraction; being nearby will do very well. For example a B&B near Chartres attracts a lot of Americans. Most tourists from the other side of the world don't stray much from the well-beaten track, but there are thousands of years of history from which to make a choice, from cave paintings to World War II; all have left their mark. Choose the location, read it up, and advertise. You should have a fairly long season, but one night stays only.

TOWNS

A large town has enough of a resident population to support a B&B even without tourists. There will always be business travellers who are fed up with hotels, and then the French themselves who visit relatives a lot and can't always be accommodated *en masse* (even if it is almost impossible to buy a sofa that isn't a put-you-up). There will also be weddings, funerals, first communions, golden weddings – to name only a few of the occasions for getting families together. People house hunting, job hunting, attending special events: there will be all sorts of reasons for them coming. Of course, all of these things happen in small places as well, but in nothing like the numbers. And if yours is a tourist town too, so much the better.

Chartres Cathedral
Decorated Grottoes of the Vézère Valley
Mont-St Michel and its Bay
Palace and Park of Versailles
Vézelay, Church and Hill
Amiens Cathedral
Cistercian Abbey of Fontenay
Palace and Park of Fontainebleau
Roman and Romanesque Monuments of Arles
Roman Theatre and its Surroundings and the 'Triumphal Arch' of Orange
Royal Saltworks of Arc-et-Senans
Place Stanislas, Place de la Carrière, and Place d'Alliance in Nancy
Church of Saint-Savin-sur-Gartempe
Cape Girolata, Cape Porto, Scandola Nature Reserve and the Piano Calanches in Corsica
Pont du Gard (Roman Aqueduct), Nimes
Strasbourg, Grand Ile
Paris, Banks of the Seine
Cathedral of Notre-Dame, Former Abbey of Saint-Rémi and Palace of Tau, Reims
Bourges Cathedral
Historic Centre of Avignon
Canal du Midi
Historic Fortified City of Carcassonne
Historic Site of Lyon
Routes of Santiago de Compostela in France
Jurisdiction of Saint-Emilion, Gironde
The Loire Valley between Sully-sur-Loire and Chalonnes-sur-Loire
Provins, Town of Medieval Fairs

Figure 1 UNESCO World heritage sites

On the outskirts (in what used to be villages) there are likely to be some streets with delightful old houses. You might even have a parking space which would be a real bonus. In the centre you will perhaps have a flat with just one or two bedrooms to let, but be very careful about the district. You won't need to provide dinner as there will be plenty of restaurants. Parking will invariably be a problem. It will be a year round business, and you may well be busier in winter than in summer, which means you could take your holiday in August like everyone else.

WHERE TO AVOID

It may seem as if most of France is a desirable location. **Not so**. There are plenty of depressing villages, suburbs and towns all over France. They just don't appear in the guide books. I stayed in a B&B where the countryside was totally flat and all you could see were electricity pylons in every direction. The B&B wasn't so great either, or was I prejudiced? I would avoid Corsica while it's politically unstable.

THE HOUSE

It's a difficult choice because there are types of house quite unknown in the UK. To start with the best: the four *épis* category requires a building with some architectural merit, or an exceptionally high standard of presentation. Even after restoration, the maintenance costs of a large old property will be enormous and the heating costs outrageous. A B&B business will only help towards the upkeep. An illustration of the scale of the problem is that I heard of a mansion sold for the equivalent of £1; in other words it was given away. Please do be **very cautious**.

For the three *épis* category the choice is wide. It could be a modern house which will be a great saving on the upkeep, but most of us foreigners prefer something old with plenty of character. If this is to be a profitable venture **do not** take on too much. An ordinary-sized house will generally be large enough for the guest bedrooms, kitchen, dining room, possibly a lounge, and accommodation for yourselves. In old farm houses you need to be aware that the ground floor was originally for the animals; the humans lived on the first floor. This means that the ground floor is low. For town houses, though they may look like three storeys from the road, they are often five storeys with a semi-basement and rooms in the roof space. A view is always a good advertising point.

Be imaginative. Could you buy two houses next door to each other, one for yourselves, and one for the guests? Or perhaps one across the road? Quirky premises are a real attention grabber too. I've seen pictures of a B&B on a barge, in a *pigeonnier* (dove cote), and in a gipsy caravan. Brilliant. There's even a guide book specially aimed at such aspects called *Chambres d'Hôtes Insolites* (Unusual Bed & Breakfasts) and published by Hachette.

What the house does need is a prettiness factor, so take some photos and see how various things will look; thatch, half-timbering, mellow stone, mature trees, courtyard and water are all winners. This, is what grabs the customers' attention. Perhaps it could be improved with some creeper here and some demolition there. It sounds cynical, but your future income is at stake.

THE LAND

The opposite situation to the house. Don't be afraid of buying all that is offered. Land is cheap in France (except in towns) and it will be a good selling point one day.

A few cautions:

1. Steeply sloping gardens make access difficult and swimming pools more expensive.

2. If agricultural land is already let, you will not be able to get possession.

3. Don't take planning permission for granted.

4. Check out the commercial neighbours for noise.

5. Is there enough room for all the parking you will need?

6. Check that there is mains drainage not too far from the building or that you can get permission for a septic tank.

7. Check that telephone, electricity and water are available if not already existing, and find out if an adsl (broadband) connection is available.

balcon (m)	balcony	maison à étage (f)	two storey house
bastide (f)	medieval village	maison de maître	master's house
bergerie (f)	sheepfold	manoir (m)	manor
château (m)	castle, mansion	mas (m)	Provence farmhouse
chaumière (f)	cottage	moulin à eau (m)	water mill
demeure (f)	home	moulin à vent	wind mill
ferme (f)	farm, farmhouse	pièce (f)	room
ferme en activitée	working farm	plan d'eau (m)	leisure lake
gentilhommière (f)	gentleman's house	randonnée (f)	hiking trail
lotissement (m)	housing estate	village perché (m)	hill town

Figure 2 Glossary

TIPS FOR MAKING IT PAY

- ◆ Choose location very carefully.
- ◆ Do not buy too large a property.
- ◆ Do buy all the land.
- ◆ Do not be too isolated if you are not used to country self sufficiency.

TIP FOR IMPROVING YOUR FRENCH

- ◆ Speak only French at meal times.

3

Buying Your Property

PEOPLE YOU ARE LIKELY TO MEET

Acheteur	Buyer (i.e. yourself)
Agent immobilier	Estate agent
Architecte	Architect
Entrepreneur	Building contractor
Expert immobilier	Buildings surveyor
Géomètre	Land surveyor
Notaire	Notary
Secrétaire	Secretary (of any of these)
Vendeur	Vendor

A DIFFERENT SYSTEM

You must not believe that buying in France is easy and straightforward, but nor must you think it is impossibly difficult. Understanding the system will allow you to plan ahead and proceed with more confidence. France has evolved a good and workable method for property purchase which cuts out most of the uncertainty experienced in the UK. The *notaire* does not perform exactly the same functions as does a solicitor in the UK. Because he acts for both parties, there is less aggravation, and since a preliminary contract is signed immediately an offer is accepted, there is almost no gazumping. It is not noticeably quicker, but when moving house, speed is not of the essence, it is certainty that matters. The French move house less frequently than we do in the UK and property is still often passed down the generations, so one's home is not seen as an investment opportunity on which to make fat profits.

ESTATE AGENT

This is a new breed in France. Traditionally, property purchase was negotiated by a *notaire* and they still handle many, but nowadays more than 50 per cent are done through estate agents as we know them. All agents based in the UK will be working in association with a French agent, but there are some British agents based only in France. Your first contacts will probably be with British agents, but once you have arrived in France call in on any local agents you see in your chosen area. Every small town has at least one. They may not be geared particularly towards foreigners, but they will have a lot of detailed local knowledge and will produce someone who speaks English if necessary. Agents' fees are not regulated, but are normally 5 per cent and are usually paid by the purchaser. In this case it will be included (and hidden) in the sale price, but check this; especially if you have negotiated the price down. Don't believe a word they say about renovation costs; get your own estimates. Naturally there are some sharks about, so check that they are members of the *Fédération Nationale des Agents Immobiliers et Mandataires/FNAIM*.

MAKING AN OFFER

Sole agencies are rare, so agents are in cut-throat competition with each other. Addresses of properties are not divulged and agents always take you there personally. You would probably never find them by yourself anyway as there are no road names in the countryside. You will have to sign that you saw the property first with them. This is so you cannot do a private deal or buy through another agent. It is a myth that there is one price for the locals and one for foreigners, the difference is that the French will bargain harder.

The time to pause is when you have seen a suitable property. If you make an offer that is accepted, the agent will try to rush you to the *notaire* at the earliest possible moment. You will sign up with only a minimum of escape clauses, and certainly no survey or estimate of any work required, though there is a seven day period in which you can withdraw without penalty. It is in the agent's interest to rush you because a delay means another could get in first and he would lose the sale. Without sole agencies there are no 'gentlemen's agreements' about not continuing to market a house under offer. This works the other way too of course, in that you could lose the property if you haven't signed. On balance it's best to be cautious and, anyway, always make an offer. We lost a very pretty property while we were thinking about it and I was very upset at the time. Since we eventually found an even better one it was for the best in the end. There are some bargains at auctions of repossessed properties, but don't attempt this unless you speak fluent French.

SURVEYOR

It is not the custom in France to have a general survey of a property done before buying. Mortgages come from banks and they are not concerned with the state of the building, only with your ability to repay the debt. They don't even hold the deeds, the *notaire* does. However, the French are gradually approaching surveys from a different angle. It is now **obligatory** to have a *dossier diagnostic technique* (technical diagnostic file) with the title deeds and it has to include surveys of the following:

◆ Lead paint – for houses built before 1949

◆ Asbestos – for houses built before 1997

◆ Termites – in certain areas

◆ Gas – for installations more than 15 years old

◆ Natural and technological hazards – in certain areas

◆ Energy performance – for information only

◆ Electricity (coming shortly).

Setting up these surveys is the responsibility of the vendor; if they are done after the *Compromis de Vente* is signed they will form *clauses suspensives* (conditions) and if any nasties are found the contract can be renogiated or it can be aborted and the deposit returned. All septic tanks in country areas are now being checked under EC regulations regarding the pollution of water supplies, so do ask about this.

Apart from the above your signature on the documents means you accept the property as it is and there is no redress for any other defects; if you want a full survey as well, then it can be included as another *clause suspensive*. You will have to set this up yourself and it will be seen as unusual.

ARCHITECT

If the house is in poor condition or you envisage doing a lot of work, then you need an architect. He will advise on the structure and also give a preliminary estimate of the cost of the work proposed. Most people think first of asking a builder for an estimate. However, without some drawings you are unlikely to be able to supply enough information for him to give anything like an accurate price. Converting an ordinary house or farm outbuildings into a mini-hotel is a complex operation. Using an architect is worthwhile even when you plan to do all the work yourself. Ask the agent for a name. There are even a few British architects practising in France.

NOTARY

This a prestigious occupation and he **and** she should be addressed as '*Maître X*'. You will have been surprised that the one *notaire* acts for both buyer and seller. Or rather the truth is he doesn't 'act' for either. He is an impartial professional whose functions are to collect the taxes, establish the correct owner, pay any mortgages, and deal with the conveyancing process. Thus he is on neither 'side'. You must accept that he is re-active and not pro-active, which means that he will obey instructions but will not give opinions. **You** must ask if there are any rights of way, service easements, fishing rights, and so on on the land, and who owns the boundary walls and fences (though I doubt if any one will actually know that). These aspects will not be shown on the deeds.

You can appoint your own *notaire* and the cost will be the same as they split the fee, but there is really no advantage. The *notaire*'s fees and the taxes will be 10–15 per cent of the purchase price, which is considerably more than in the UK. If the *notaire*'s office is near your property, it is a good idea to meet at least once in the process; you may need some advice in the future and it may even be given without charge. However, they rarely speak English.

If a *notaire* is the selling agent, then this is the one time when it would be best to appoint someone else yourself.

PRELIMINARY CONTRACT *(Compromis de vente)*

Your offer has been accepted and in the UK you never see the estate agent again. In France the agent will stay with you right through to completion. Discuss any *clauses suspensives* you want to include in the preliminary contract.

Some possible conditional clauses:

◆ Obtaining a mortgage.
◆ A satisfactory survey.
◆ Selling a previous house.
◆ Obtaining a *certificat d'urbanisme* (preliminary planning permission).
◆ Permission for swimming pool or septic tank.
◆ Confirmation of the land area.
◆ Possibility of drainage, water, or electricity connections if none existing.

They must be agreed with the vendor and if there are too many he could refuse or conclude that you are not a serious buyer and pull out altogether. If the business is to be run as a company, then the company should buy the property as it will be expensive to change afterwards. As long as this is noted, the exact name can be added later. There is a form of company known as *Société Civile Immobilière/SCI* which is a property holding company only and is practical when several people are buying, though they all need to be resident in France as the British tax on this is not favourable. Discuss the matter with the *notaire* because it's a complicated area. Also discuss inheritance because French law prevails whatever a will says. It is possible to register a business in the UK if there is a British based partner and address; this will avoid some items of French legislation. Take advice on this from an international lawyer.

If your project depends on renovating old agricultural buildings it is vital to include the *certificat d'urbanisme.* Permission to change the use to a habitation is much harder to obtain than it was until quite recently. What will you do with a vast barn otherwise?

You will be expected to sign the preliminary contract as soon as possible, usually within a week of your offer. You can insist on having a bilingual lawyer check the contract, and it can be signed by proxy, but it really is better if you can attend in person. The agent will be there, and if the vendor is as well then any last minute changes to the contract can be made swiftly. The *notaire* will obtain a *certificat d'urbanisme* if requested; any other conditions you must deal with yourself. The date for completion will be set (normally 60 or 90 days) but can be otherwise by agreement. Now is the time to open a French bank account as you must pay a deposit of 10–15 per cent of the purchase price.

LAND REGISTRY PLAN *(Plan Cadastral)*

All parcels of land are numbered and shown on this official plan and a copy will be attached to the deeds. If there is any doubt about a boundary, or you are not buying the whole parcel, or a *droit de passage* (right of way) has to be established, then a *géomètre* (land surveyor) has to be employed. He will set pegs in the ground to mark the boundaries and prepare a new plan if necessary. This is an excellent system as his word is law, and it avoids the squabbles over 15cm of land we suffer in the UK. The *notaire* will set up the visit and, as always, be present if you can.

FIXTURES AND FITTINGS

French owners have a tendency to go off with the fittings. Kitchen cabinets, wood burning stoves, you name it, they have all been known to disappear. Even the pendant lights have been snipped off 5cm below the ceiling. I hope they forgot to switch off the electricity before they did it! Of course you can make formal lists, but a better idea is to go and confront them and ask if they are taking anything. Have the agent along as a witness if possible and that should put a stop to it.

COMPLETION *(Acte authentique)*

If you want to cancel the sale and have not given notice three days before the completion date that a *clause suspensive* has not been met, then you will lose the deposit and probably have to pay the agent's fee as well. Or you could be compelled to complete. So you are probably going to go ahead. If you want a draft copy of the final sale document in advance, you will have to ask for it. You may want to take the wise precaution of having a bilingual professional check it for you. A big expense here is transferring sterling from your British bank to the *notaire* in euros. A good exchange rate makes a big difference on such a large sum. Specialist foreign exchange brokers, such as Currencies Direct, Foreign Currency Direct, HIFX and Moneycorp, offer better terms than banks. For example, on transferring £150,000 the saving could be as much as £6,000. Set up the arrangements in good time to avoid a bridging loan. You are expected to be present at the signing but, again, it can be done by proxy. The *notaire* keeps the deeds even when there is a mortgage, and you will receive a copy a couple of months later.

TAKING POSSESSION

The theoretical time for taking possession is midday on the day of the sale. This really means *14 heures* (2pm) as you are now a French property-owner and will need a good lunch. You will have to get used to the 24-hour clock too. You will need to contact the water, gas, electricity and telephone companies immediately to have the meters read and the accounts put into your name. If they are cut off there will be substantial re-connection charges. All property **must** have third party liability insurance.

TIPS FOR MAKING IT PAY

◆ Understand the difference between the British and French systems of conveyancing.

- If necessary, have conditional clauses for permissions, electricity and water services in case there are any problems.

- Make sure the previous owners don't take away all the fixtures and fittings.

TIP FOR IMPROVING YOUR FRENCH

- Listen to the BBC World Service in French.

4

Renovating Your Property

THE PEOPLE YOU WILL MEET

Charpentier	Carpenter and joiner
Couvreur	Roofer
Electricien	Electrician
Entrepreneur	Builder
Maçon	Mason, bricklayer
Peintre	Painter and decorator
Plombier	Plumber

HOUSE IN GOOD CONDITION

You have decided to let a couple of spare bedrooms either in a house you already own or one bought recently with B&B in mind. There will be little or even no work required unless there aren't enough bathrooms. However, if you have just bought the house, you could easily find there are hidden problems and all is not as good as it looked on the surface. You must be warned that many French houses are not maintained to the standards we expect in the UK. One reason is the absence of building regulations as we know them in the UK. This is relevant to recent buildings and any work done to older buildings. Another reason is the absence of the surveys insisted on by building societies in the UK.

Problem areas

It's quite down market these days to have a resident family and guests sharing a bathroom, so there's really got to be an en-suite for every guest bedroom. Adding bathrooms will be a major expense and may mean sacrificing a bedroom; the cost of building an extension simply to use it for a a bathroom will never be recovered from running a B&B. Similarly, in rented premises building work is unlikely to be worthwhile and may not be allowed anyway.

Even as little as two bedrooms can mean six more people in addition to the resident family and it will put extra load on the services; your electricity, water heater and septic tank could all prove inadequate. For this reason, and for the safety of your guests, it is wise to have a diagnostic test of each of the services as breakdowns can lead to embarrassing confrontations.

Rest of house

There is very little more that is absolutely essential, apart from making the house generally look well cared for and inviting. If the visitors' rooms are on the ground floor, could they have a separate entrance? Breakfasts will not present any problem as they can be out-of-doors, or even taken to the bedrooms, as well as at the usual dining-table. A popular option for meals is to build a conservatory (in the north of the country) or a veranda (in the south) and either of these will increase the value of the house.

OLD HOUSES NEEDING RESTORATION

Knowing Brits, it is more likely you have bought an old house that needs a lot doing to it. The French think we are quite mad and they prefer new houses for their main home, but will take on an old house in the country as a second home. Then they more or less camp there without restoring it.

You have bought an old house for its charm and character, yet have got to bring it to modern standards of comfort and sanitation. Nevertheless, work out a budget and **stick to it**. At the extreme it has been known for restoration work to cost **three times** the amount budgeted. If you spend too much, you will never make a profit on a B&B or get your money back when you sell. But the trouble with the B&B business is that standards are rising all the time. What looked adequate at the time of building may not be so ten years later. And all building work should last at least a decade. Therefore you have got to keep a sharp eye on the costs, but at the same time maintain a good standard. Also remember that when you have spent money doing up an old house, don't imagine that you now have the equivalent of a new one; the maintenance will be continuous. Address your questions about planning permissions to, and obtain forms from, the *Direction Départmental d'Equipement/DDE* (public works department). There are no fees and your application will be dealt with swiftly – that is unless you are in a listed historic building, in which case things will take much longer and you will be informed of the hurdles.

Existing features
To retain the authenticity, do restore the features that give it character, not forgetting the smaller items like ironmongery and stone sinks. It is all a great expense, but afford it if you can because it is your business asset (*see Fig. 3*). Having spent the money, these antique structures need a new use. *Pigeonniers* are useful for the pool machinery, as part of a *gîte*, or how about a laundry for the guests? Bread ovens look interesting when sprayed white inside and lit, old machinery should be kept if possible. Whatever it is, be imaginative and make a feature of it.

Replanning
You are not stuck with the same use of rooms as found existing. Ground floors are often rather gloomy and can be improved by moving the dining/lounge area towards the back and then opening it up to the garden. Existing kitchens can be very small, and I don't know how the French

Window with shutters

Pigeonnier

Bread oven door

Barn

Front door

Figure 3   Always preserve existing features

produce gourmet meals; it really needs to be of a good size to accommodate a *table d'hôte*. Should the stairs be moved to a more convenient position? How about dividing the house horizontally so that the guests have one floor and you have the other? Do remember here that a bedroom on the ground floor will be appreciated by elderly people and is also essential for disabled guests (ask whatever organisation you belong to for detailed requirements for the disabled). Can an existing bathroom be re-arranged to open off a bedroom instead of a corridor? Don't be constrained by what is there now.

Minimum Room Sizes:

	Bedroom for Two	Bedroom for Three	Bathroom
Three *épis*	14m^2	17m^2	4m^2
Four *épis*	18m^2	17m^2	5m^2

NOTIFICATION OF MINOR WORK *(Déclaration de Travaux)*

Only minor work to the exterior of buildings needs to be declared. Very small items, such as terraces, walls up to 2m high, or any constructions less than 2m square and 1.5m high, are totally exempt. A simple notification **is** all that is required for small constructions such as sheds and greenhouses under 35m square, extensions under 20m square, and minor work to an existing building such as new doors and windows and also for swimming pools (though pools are subject to other regulations). The submission is simple enough to do yourself and the merest sketch or diagram to accompany the form is sufficient.

PRELIMINARY PLANNING PERMISSION *(Certificat d'Urbanisme)*

This is required for a new detached building or when a detached building used for anything other than habitation is to be converted to a dwelling. A B&B is considered to be a habitation, and a certificate is not required for a structure physically joined onto a house such as a garage or barn. There are two conditions, but even if met they don't automatically guarantee permission:

1. The land must be zoned for building on the town map. If not so zoned you can always try but don't be surprised by a refusal.

2. The site must have access and be capable of connections to the services.

I trust that, if this is crucial to your business plans, you instructed the *notaire* to obtain the permission before buying the property. If not, you should be able to cope yourself as it consists of little more than filling in the form and supplying location and site plans. It is valid for two years and you should not assume it will automatically be renewed if it lapses.

PLANNING PERMISSION *(Permis de Construire)*

The above permissions do not allow you to build. Now you need the *Permis de Construire*. This is required for new buildings, major exterior alterations, extensions over 20 square metres and demolition. You must supply a set of drawings with plans sections and elevations, photos of the site and any existing buildings, location and site plans, details of water supply and drainage, notes of the exterior materials, and of course lengthy forms. **And** if the building is over 170m^2 in area (about the size of a three-bedroom house) the drawings must be signed by a French-registered architect. This limit applies even for conversion of only part of the building. I recommend that you should have professional help.

However, you may reckon you have the necessary skills. Obtain the forms and comply with them scrupulously. There is, incredibly, a free service provided by the *Centre d'Architecture, d'Urbanisme et d'Environnement/CAUE* where an architect will examine the drawings and give advice prior to submission. This may well save a refusal. As in the UK, a refusal is hard to reverse.

Do not start work without the permission. It only lasts for two years, and if it is about to run out start the work in some small way. Consult with the town hall for a historically listed building.

BUILDING REGULATIONS

For carrying out the work you, or your builder, must:

◆ Display the required board.
◆ Notify when work has started.
◆ Notify when work has finished.

The system is quite different from that in the UK. Detailed drawings of the work are not submitted and there are no inspections during the course of building. However, regulations do exist and are called *Code de la Construction et de l'Habitation.* Compliance is the builder's responsibility and insurance is obligatory. Obviously there are strict regulations for all the services, but they are administered by the companies concerned.

USING AN ARCHITECT

When to use an architect

If the restoration work is minor you will make your own decisions. When it involves major structural work, substantial re-planning of the inside, and certainly if you are practically gutting the place, then please do use an architect. Why do all that work and yet not make the very best use of the building? Obviously I would say that since I am one myself. Well here is a small example of the kind of benefit. I complimented a proprietor on the way he had converted a double bedroom into a family room by adding a mezzanine going up into the roof space. He said, 'The architect thought of that.' Honest, he didn't know I'm one myself.

The architect's work

This is to obtain all necessary permissions and, if engaged, take the project to completion; in which case he will find and conduct all negotiations with builders. One of his tasks is to keep the project within budget. In inexperienced hands the cost can mount to alarming heights and an architect's fee will have been more than spent. Visit two or three firms and discuss fees – they should preferably be located near the project. Usually the first visit is free; if a scheme is aborted there will be a charge. You will be expected to sign a contract. If you are doing the building work yourself an architect can be employed to do the drawings and get the permission but it is not necessary always to have the full service.

LARGE BUILDING PROJECTS

General contractor *(Entreprise Générale de Bâtiment)*

The normal method of building is to employ each trade separately. This poses problems if you do not speak French and have absolutely no experience of building, or will be absent much of the time. If any of these apply it is better to employ a general contractor, though it will cost a little more.

By employing a local builder to do some immediate work, which included a new bathroom and septic tank, we managed to welcome the first paying guest three months after we arrived, and the business was up and running.

We employed mostly French workmen and found them competent and hard-working. Nothing ever got finished on time – so what's new? We also used some English builders and one Australian. The advantage there is that you can take up references as their clients will also be mainly ex-pats.

The criteria for choosing builders is **not** the same as for private work. They must be prompt, must clean up, and must finish everything completely. These attributes are more important than saving the last sou. Finding builders when you first arrive is difficult. Ask your neighbours, or ask the estate agent who sold you the house. If you take a name from the *Yellow Pages*, ask for their *SIRET* number. If they have one they are properly registered. General contractors are always likely to sub-contract some work; don't liase directly with such a firm, it's entirely the builder's responsibility.

For all building work you must realise that if you go home, they will. There are goats to tend, chickens to feed, and all manner of other urgent jobs. So, if possible, you should stay around or try to visit at least once a fortnight, or have someone else do so and report on progress. Builders will start at 8am and take a two-hour lunch break at 12.00. Like everyone else, they are bound to the 35-hour week unless self employed. Do not proffer mugs of tea or coffee; it is not the custom. Sunday is the day for the family, therefore business calls are not welcome.

Paying

Never pay the whole sum in advance, but you will probably be asked for a deposit of 15 per cent and some money as the work progresses if it is extensive. For a private householder the *TVA* is 5.5 per cent for renovation, but this rate does not apply to materials bought for DIY. Otherwise for building work and materials *TVA* is 19.6 per cent, which will be refunded in full for a *TVA* registered business. It is expected that you will raise queries on the final bill, but you must get a reputation as a **prompt payer**, or no one will work for you.

Insurance

When the work is finished, it will be guaranteed for one year. After that the builder **must** have insurance to cover the work for defects. It runs for ten years for structural work, two years for other work, and one year for alterations. If you have set up a substantial amount of work without professional help, you are advised to have insurance yourself to cover an expert handling any claims on your behalf.

MINOR BUILDING PROJECTS

Assuming the amount of building work is not large and you are not doing it all yourself, then you will be engaging the various tradesmen. Your biggest problem will be keeping to a budget. The causes of increased costs are:

◆ Not giving complete and clear instructions.
◆ Not getting firm quotations.
◆ Last minute changes.
◆ Delays of your own making.
◆ Unforeseen problems.

The latter can only be solved by keeping some money back for contingencies. The remainder are entirely your own fault.

Instructions

If a builder doesn't know precisely what you want, he can't prepare an accurate quotation. If you are without professional help, prepare a 'shopping list' of what is required. List it room by room, very simply, i.e. 'new window'. At the end, list all the items you are going to buy yourself. If it needs to be in French, I'm sure errors of grammar will be forgiven.

Quotations *(Devis)*

If you can, ask two or three people to quote (if you can find that many). If no reply arrives within a fortnight, chase it; it looks businesslike. The builder should submit two copies of the quotation. He will have signed the original; you then sign and return it, and it becomes the contract. The snag with this system is the quotation is often only six sentences long, when it would take several closely printed pages to specify the work properly. All you can do is question him closely on the extent of the work and what is included. If major items seem to be missing, don't be afraid to ask him to re-submit the quotation, and don't accept a verbal reply. It should have stated the time for the work; it won't be kept to but is a help when progress is slow. We found tradesmen generally willing to return and attend to any small problems after the work is completed.

Changes

Make up your mind. Changes made after receipt of the quotation leave you wide open to substantial extra costs. Even small alterations have repercussions you never realised.

Delays

It is quite normal for you to buy some items direct such as sanitary fittings, wood burning stove, wall tiles, but you will not get a trade discount and will pay TVA at 19.6 per cent, so it's not always worthwhile. Any ordering must be done in good time. If a builder has to wait, it will cost extra. Check if delivery is included because quite often it isn't. Some shops have vans for hire or take it in your own vehicle if possible. We came home one day with a bath on the roof rack; we simply didn't want to miss a special offer!

BUILDING-IT-YOURSELF

Competence

Do not take on too much. You have come to France to run a B&B, not to learn the building trade. One thing is certain: it will take longer. I have known it take three years before the first paying guest arrived. Of course it is cheaper, but you have lost all that period of income. Try and phase the work by finishing a couple of bedrooms and the dining-room first. Then do later phases by closing for the winter when there's hardly anyone about anyway and work can proceed unhindered. In southern France even outside work can continue through the winter. Building is dangerous work – did you see the programme on TV a while back about the chap who cut off his own hand (they sewed it back on)? Do take care. Amateurs always find it hard to work to a deadline, but the cement mixer and materials must be cleared away by the end of April.

Assistance

You will need to employ tradesmen for some of the work. A French electrician is **essential**, probably also roofer, plasterer, and plumber. Do not bring over your British mates; it does not go down well. The thrifty Dutch have the reputation of bringing all their workmen and materials. The caustic comment is 'they even bring their own sandwiches'. Use reputable trades persons and try your utmost to avoid disputes; if you tangle with French law you are unlikely to get a result that will be satisfactory for you.

Materials

Paint is cheaper in Britain, but otherwise do not bring your own materials. In particular, water pipe sizes and therefore sanitary fitting waste outlets are **not** the same. I heard one French person curse the previous British owner of his house for using a product for which a replacement part was unobtainable because it was not sold in France.

The French, too, are very keen on *bricolage* (DIY) and there are plenty of well-stocked shops; some are vast emporiums. There are also sanitary fitting suppliers with vast stocks, general builders' merchants, timber yards, and specialist joinery shops. Unfortunately, as a newcomer and a foreigner, you may not at first get the discounts a builder would normally expect. If you establish a good relationship with a smaller supplier, they will give much more helpful advice than the big chains. Go to www.francethisway.com/renovation/diyinfrance.html for help with buying materials and general advice for novice builders.

Building practice

To suit differing climates, every country constructs their houses accordingly and you will have to find out French methods. France still has excellent stonemasons and joiners with very high standards of craftsmanship. But bricklaying is not their forte. The organisation *Maisons Paysannes de France* will give a lot of advice on renovating old buildings (see their address in Useful Addresses).

THE BUILDING WORK

Get the priorities right. This is a true story: the previous owners had put in a new bathroom with a pink suite including his'n'hers washbasins. Very posh if you like pink. But the drain went to a ditch.

Structural work inside and out	Drainage
Re-building chimneys	Timber treatment
Re-roofing and new gutters	New stairs
Plan for new bathrooms even if not to be built yet	Sandblasting inside

Figure 4   This work MUST be done first

Some work can be done later, but remember that all building work makes a mess.

New doors and windows	Plastering and floor finishes
New partitions	Central heating and insulation
Pointing stone and brickwork	Fitting out bathrooms and kitchens
Extensions	

Figure 5   This work can be done later

Roof

Tiled roofs originally had oak boarding and hand-made tiles which are very heavy. It is a kindness to old timbers to lighten the load with modern interlocking tiles but they do not look authentic. If possible, use clay tiles made to the traditional shapes. Thatch should be replaced with matching materials. Chimneys are often in a bad state and need complete re-building. Country houses originally did not have gutters but they have usually been added, town houses now all have gutters. Look in heavy rain for leaks.

Exterior walls

For new walls, the ideal is to match the original stone or brick. Nowadays they have an inside skin of *brique* (insulated clay bricks); cavity walls are not used. If you really cannot afford this, then it will have to be the modern standard of *brique* with rendering outside. Some very old brick walls are built of sun-dried bricks, and, because these are so weak, they usually have the corners and openings reinforced with fired bricks. These soft bricks cannot be left without rendering. For repairs to exposed brickwork, always use reclaimed bricks. Old stone and brick walls may need re-pointing. Be careful here, as if amateurishly done, it can spoil the look of the whole building. Damp-proof courses are a late nineteenth-century invention and I do not know of any satisfactory way of inserting them in stone or timber frame walls; brick walls can be dealt with by specialists.

For damp walls, the water has to be stopped either with a land drain outside or waterproofing inside, or both. The trouble with farm houses is that originally the ground floor was for the animals, and the humans lived on the first floor all nice and dry. So for any part of the house which is below ground and for damp basements, you will have to call on specialists. New openings should have lintels to match those existing and windows should have a vertical proportion, not the modern horizontal. A good mason will make new openings and move existing ones in brickwork or stone so that you will hardly know the work has been done – at a cost of course.

Floors

Really old houses had beaten earth on the lowest floor, but probably something has been done by now, even if only paving on top of the earth. A new concrete slab gives the opportunity to include a damp-proof membrane and insulation. On upper floors old oak beams with 2cm thick boards are the epitome of character. Not much of this boarding has survived to the present century. It is possible to replace bad areas with second-hand boards, but you will have to accept uneven floors and propping under the furniture legs to make them stand evenly. The problem with replacing oak boards with modern thin pine is that the beams are too far apart. Either you have to accept a bouncy floor or move the beams closer together.

Sound insulation of wood floors is difficult and is a particular problem if one bedroom is above another. Thick carpets are one solution, or have the new laminated planks, but they must be laid on a 7mm insulating underlay. Buy good quality and have it properly laid.

A bathroom above a bedroom is an even worse problem. A solution is to raise it a step. The space is filled with insulation and it has the added benefit of making the pipe runs easier. But the WC flushing in the small hours will still be heard. If the whole structure of the floor has to be replaced, consider the system of pre-cast concrete T-shaped beams with blocks laid in between and screed on top. This is ultra-modern construction but gives excellent sound insulation between floors and total freedom of choice of finish on top.

Timber pests

Woodworm and death watch beetle are rife in France. Treat the timbers before any other work, and again later, and again. But the pests are only kept at bay, not eliminated. Termites have appeared in some areas but the previous owners will have had a compulsory inspection in the three months before the sale of the property. If you suspect dry rot, call in the experts.

Doors, windows, shutters

There may be original doors; if so, keep them. Otherwise, please do not have flush doors; they look so cheap and out of character. Doors come complete with frames, hinges, lock, and glazing where required. Windows are unlikely to be original, so it is a matter of their condition and your pocket if you replace them. Windows also come complete with ironmongery and glazing. Only have double glazing if you are having new windows anyway; it does not pay to change. Choose windows with glazing bars to match the original ones; big panes look very modern. All windows open inwards so that you can reach the shutters, and the French will expect working shutters to the bedrooms. They have the double purpose of keeping the sun out (in which case they should be latched slightly open) or as double glazing (when they should be fully shut). If any of this joinery has to be purpose-made to special sizes, which is very likely, there are excellent joinery works. Window frames should be of wood, not plastic or metal. If more light is needed it looks better to add another window than to enlarge an existing one, excepting that windows are not too difficult to take down to the ground to form a door.

Stairs

Old stairs will either be grandiose or miserably steep and narrow, but if it is worth keeping (even though rickety) an experienced carpenter can probably stabilise it. If a new flight is necessary, don't have winders (tapered treads) as shown in the glossy joinery brochures and which are common in French houses. They are dangerous for children and not suitable for adults carrying luggage. If the stair needs to change direction, have a ¼ or ½ landing. Have a firm handrail for the whole flight, and no opening in the balustrade should be more than 11cm (so that children can't get their heads through).

Inside walls

If load bearing, they will be *brique* again. Do not replace load bearing walls with a beam without professional help. Partitions these days are of metal stud and plasterboard. If between bedrooms or bedroom and bathroom, then the space between the studs should be filled with glass wool for sound insulation. This gives some improvement, but good sound insulation is impossible to achieve in old buildings. Old plaster may need replacing because it is loose or soft. The walls can be lined with plaster board, but this gives a very modern feel. In really old houses it's better to re-render, following the less-than-straight contours of the existing wall. Stone walls internally can be sand-blasted. This looks superb but is laborious because it will need re-pointing afterwards. Possibly do this on the ground floor only.

Heating

If you intend to stay open in the winter, then you **must** have central heating even in the south. The winters are certainly shorter there but are still cold. Oil has rocketed in price lately but as mains gas is only available in towns you may have no choice. Underfloor heating has come back into favour, but it has a slow warm-up period which is a disadvantage to a B&B.

Open fires are for ambience, not serious heating. Wood-burning stoves are more economical but a lot of work and do not heat the whole house. If you have not got central heating, it will have to be electricity; check out oil-filled radiators and storage heaters; they are improving all the time. The fuse board can be set up so that the electric heaters cut out first if the system is overloaded. An overload is very likely on a cold morning in a B&B when everyone is getting up and everything is on all at once. Insulate the loft space of course. A word of warning on insulation: mice find polystyrene very cosy too and we cursed the day we ever allowed the stuff in the house.

Heating large double-height spaces such as a converted barn is difficult because there is just not enough wall space for the number of radiators required. The best method is a warm air system such as is found in small village halls. You would find heating a big space like this just for a couple of breakfasts to be totally uneconomic.

Solar energy has not yet become commonplace in France, but you could consider it as you need a lot of heating and hot water. There is even a government grant, so ask a specialist installer for details. But do site the panels discreetly if on an old roof.

Water

The water supply has been privatised and there are several companies. In some areas it is very hard. All water is metered. There never were water tanks in the roof space so you won't find them even in older houses. Healthwise it is drinkable from the tap; tastewise it is a matter of preference.

You need **plenty** of hot water. The peak time is just before dinner. People have just arrived, or are changing for dinner, or putting tots to bed. Everyone in fact is bathing or showering all at once, so a big well-insulated cylinder is essential. If run from the central heating boiler, it will cost ⅔ less than electricity. The very well-insulated cylinders are usually situated in the roof space; airing cupboards are unknown. If space is really difficult to find for a normal cylinder, there are pressurized types, but they are a job for an expert only. Be scrupulous about insulating pipes because a freeze-up will bring the business to a standstill.

Electricity

The monopoly is still part government owned, though that is likely to change. The company is *Electricité de France/EDF.* The voltage is 220/230 the same as the UK, but the wiring system is entirely different. **Do not** have a British electrician install a ring main circuit. The electricity company will refuse to connect, and it is extremely dangerous to a French electrician working on the installation in the future. A disadvantage of the system is that the location of heavy-duty appliances such as dishwashers, washing machines and heaters have to be specified in advance. But an advantage of the system is that shavers and hair dryers can be run from the light fitting over the basin without further provision. Internal bathrooms and WCs need mechanical ventilation and it can be noisy. Electricity is cheaper than in many other countries because of the huge amount generated by atomic power stations, and because most of the power lines are overhead. This latter makes for more cuts to the supply than we are used to.

Gas

The company is *Gaz de France/GDF* and is a joint company, *EDF/GDF*, with the electricity company. Mains gas is available in towns only. Elsewhere you can have a large cylinder placed outdoors or even underground – only worth it for central heating. Or you can have two cylinders outside near the point of use and with an automatic changeover. **Do not** have the small cylinders positioned under the worktop as they need changing manually. You have to remember to keep a spare and they run out at the most inconvenient times. **Do not** have a local gas water heater where there is a shower, because they require different water pressures.

Drainage

In conurbations you will be connected to main drainage just as in Britain. Don't worry if it has to be pumped uphill; it's a not uncommon necessity. In the country you will have a septic tank. Don't worry about it; they are really no trouble. For a B&B it's most unlikely that an existing installation will be large enough. For a new one the rules are much stricter than they used to be because of fears of pollution. You will need an *étude* (study) to assess the impact of the proposed tank, then you will need permission. It is best left in the hands of a specialist builder who will get the permission and do the work. The main thing is to build a large enough one to cope with any future expansion.

Accommodating 10cm waste pipes from newly added WCs is a major problem; they are unsightly if draped over the exterior, and noisy and ugly inside. Think this through before starting **any** other work. **Do not** install a *broyeur* (electric shredder) to solve this situation. They are noisy and hellish to clean when blocked.

Children's safety

All glass in windows and doors below 90cm height should be safety glass or have protective film applied (this film is available in DIY stores). Any upstairs window sills below 90cm height should have a balustrade outside to prevent children climbing out; these are usually wrought iron and actually look very decorative.

Disabled provision

The bedroom and its en-suite shower room **must** be on the ground floor, with level or easy ramped access from the parking area to the room and dining room. Ask whatever organisation you belong to for guidance and the detailed requirements.

ardoise (f)	slate	isolation (f)	insulation
amiante (m)	asbestos	linteau (m)	lintel
béton (m)	concrete	livraison (f)	delivery
béton armé	reinforced concrete	mansarde (f)	loft
bois exotique (m)	hardwood	marche (f)	step
bricolage (m)	do-it-yourself	mazout (f)	heating oil
brique (m)	brick	menuiserie (f)	joinery
carreau (m)	wall/floor tile	peinture (f)	paint
carrelage (m)	tiling	peinture acrylique	emulsion paint
chaudière (f)	boiler	persienne (f)	louvred shutter
chauffage (m)	heating	pierre (f)	stone
chauffage central	central heating	pin (m)	pine
chaume (m)	thatch	plafond (m)	ceiling
cheminée (f)	chimney	plancher (m)	floor
couche (f)	coat (of paint)	plâtre (m)	plaster
crépi (m)	textured coating	porte (f)	door
devis (m)	estimate	porte fenêtre	French window
électricité (m)	electricity	porte d'entrée	front door
électrique	electric	pouter (f)	beam
escalier (m)	stairs	prise (f)	electric socket
escabeau (m)	step-ladder	quinquaillerie (f)	ironmongery
(à l')étage	on the first floor	radiateur (m)	radiator
fenêtre (f)	window	rez-de-chaussée (m)	ground floor
fiche (f)	electric plug	robinet d'arrêt (m)	stopcock
fil (m)	wire	traveaux (f)	building work
fosse (m)	ditch	tuile (f)	roof tile
fosse septique	septic tank	tuyau (m)	pipe
four à pain (m)	bread oven	vitre (f)	pane of glass
gaz (m)	gas	vitrage (f)	glazing
gouttière (f)	gutter	double vitrage	double glazing
interrupteur (m)	switch	volet (m)	shutter

Figure 6 Glossary

TIPS FOR MAKING IT PAY

- Employ an architect to get the best out of your building.

- Get firm quotations from builders.

- Do not take on too much DIY.

TIP FOR IMPROVING YOUR FRENCH

- Read a French newspaper such as *Le Monde* or *Le Figaro*.

5

Designing the Interior

AMBIENCE

Why stay in a B&B? What else is there? There are:

Chain hotels – blandly uniform, see one and you've seen them all; totally impersonal

Small family run hotels – quality varies, some absolutely delightful, some dreadful

Large hotels – at the cheaper end impersonal, at the luxury level superb

Therefore, to be an attractive alternative to the competition, a B&B has to have a welcoming, friendly, individual atmosphere, but yet not be **so** homely that paying guests feel embarrassed to be intruding in someone else's private life. It's quite difficult to get the right balance between formality and informality, so my advice is to err on the side of formality. Keep the rooms free of too much personal clutter. Obviously most of the furniture will be pieces you already have, but you will find that much of it isn't suitable, and you should be ruthless about discarding any that looks tired and can't be freshened up. New furniture should be stout and serviceable, but avoid plastic, metal and chipboard as much as possible and keep to wood for a warmer feeling. It has to be admitted that a few B&Bs let the side down badly, and French hotel wallpaper has a world reputation for awfulness.

buanderie (f)	utility room	salle de bain (f)	bathroom
cave (f)	cellar	salle de jeux (f)	games room
chambre (f)	bedroom	salle à manger (f)	dining room
couloir (m)	corridor	salon (m)	lounge
cuisine (f)	kitchen	sous-sol (m)	basement
grenier (m)	attic	toilettes (f)	lavatory
placard (m)	cupboard	veranda (f)	veranda
salle d'eau (f)	shower room	vestibule (m)	hall

Figure 7   The rooms

STYLE

For a B&B of course you'll not need to buy all new furniture, but it does need a lot more than a three bedroom house. So give the matter some thought and work towards a coherent look. Style is an emotive subject.

The choice is easy for a new house, as it will surely look better with modern furniture. The 1950s to 1970s stripped pine and Habitat look isn't old enough to be fashionable yet, so keep it mostly modern. But 1930s art deco (all jazzy angles and chrome) is **the** trend of the moment and prices are therefore high in the auction rooms, though the machine finishes are difficult to restore to good condition after 70 years. You need to have a keen eye for the correct furniture and wallpapers for the whole effect not to look like a junk shop. Period furniture is generally taken to be what the British call Victorian – in the trade it's called 'brown'. It's lost the cachet it had until recently and prices have dropped. You may have large rooms and high ceilings in which case it is appropriate. Much prized in France are the enormous *armoires* (cupboards) which can come with the house as they are literally often too big to move. If a steep price is demanded say 'no' – it may well be left behind anyway as it would probably disintegrate if moved. The delicate style that we commonly called Regency and the French call Louis XIV (not correctly but never mind) is too valuable to have genuine pieces in a B&B, so they'll need to be reproductions. This look is very popular in the right house. The French love the pretty fabrics and wallpapers known as *Toile de Jouy*. Go to www.toiledejouy.com.fr to see some samples. Genuine peasant and medieval items are so rare as to be unlikely to be the real thing. Even with a period style it is sophisticated to have one striking modern piece. Or why not have modern chairs with the old refectory table you did manage to find?

Whatever the choice you're not a museum and it's not possible to be completely in the style of an old house. So why not make a clean break in your old stone farmhouse and paint the walls white and have all modern furniture with just one or two antiques? But beware that neither the guests, their children, nor the cleaning lady will be as careful with them as you would wish.

HOW TO ACQUIRE THE FURNITURE

Where will you source the extra stuff? First put the word around your relatives and friends about your plans and you'll be surprised what turns up. Next go to furniture auctions in the UK, as they will have bankrupt stock as well as the usual throw-outs. The French *brocantes* (open air antique markets) seem generally to have outrageous prices but there may be something useful. Further down the scale are car boot sales, with pure wool blankets thrown out in favour of duvets. The French equivalent of the car boot sale is the *vide grenier* (empty attic sale), and one thing they commonly have is large old picture frames. These can be cleaned and painted. Hobby shops stock kits for making up damaged mouldings. For new furniture there are plenty of stores in France that are the equivalent of MFI – choose **very** carefully. There's also an Ikea in most cities, if you've got the necessary skill for assembling flat packs. At the top end of the market is Roche Bobois, which is much too expensive for a B&B but do go along to pinch a few ideas.

Avoid clutter but give the establishment some character by displaying your personal interests; they make a good talking point. Put on show any previous sporting trophies or photos, or items from hobbies or jobs. Enlarge a photo of your great grandparents and put it in a heavy fame. Confine the pictures to those you appreciate yourself, then make a really positive statement by having them large or perhaps five or six in a row – something that will dominate the room.

Some practical points:

♦ Fix **everything** securely: mirrors, pictures, handrails.

♦ **Do not** have too many notices or you'll look like a dragon of a seaside landlady.

♦ Breakable items such as vases, lamps, ornaments **will get broken**, so don't put out the family heirlooms

BEDROOMS

Beds

For one room, you'd better have twin beds. For two, three, or four rooms, have one room with twin beds and the rest double. For five or six rooms have two twin and the rest double. If the room is large enough, then one double and one single is a good combination and is called a family room, but it can also be let as either a double or a twin room. We had two family rooms, in fact one was large enough to take a folding bed as well, and during the summer holiday, they were filled from end to end with a family, but the rest of the year they were just double bedrooms. Single rooms are not worth it unless you have a room so small that it will only take a single bed, because they need a shower room the same size as a double room.

Although most British and French couples opt for a double bed, some nationalities such as American, German, Scandinavian and Japanese prefer twin beds. The Dutch like large beds, single or double, since they are tall people.

French beds are the same standard sizes as British ones:

Single	90 × 190cm
Double	140 × 190cm
Queen	150 × 200cm
King	160 × 200cm

If you have a small room adjoining the main bedroom or a mezzanine, which is designated only for children, then you could have 80cm-wide single beds or bunks, otherwise these are considered sub-standard. A width of 80cm is acceptable for a folding bed as that is also only for children. You will need a cot, though it won't often be used as most people bring their own.

Good quality beds and mattresses (sprung please) are **essential**, so how come some proprietors miss out? Bed heads are necessary; they can be fixed to the wall instead of the bed and are quite easy to make for yourself, but anything at the foot only slows the bed making.

For the grade four level you should consider the larger bed sizes and the possibility of a four poster or one of the many varieties of canopy. The room should be limited to two people; it is expected that children will have a separate room.

Other furnishing

The contents of hotel rooms are very carefully considered, and B&B owners can learn a lot from them. Before the guests arrive, the room should look just a touch on the empty side because you'll be amazed at what clients bring in these people carriers. Wardrobes are best built in; freestanding ones collect cobwebs behind and are a bother if the floor isn't 100 per cent level. They don't need to be large. A single door width provides enough hanging space, but shelves for clothes in the same cupboard are better than a chest of drawers as they can be checked at a glance for things left behind. Have a table rather than a dressing-table, then it does for writing as well, with a stool or chair. Guests spend a lot of time in the bedroom so it needs to be comfortable. If there's room, have a couple of small arm chairs; they can be wicker, otherwise it'll have to be a couple of ordinary chairs. If you do have a chest of drawers, it needs a piece of 5mm glass with polished edges for the top, as both alcohol and beauty products leave stains. Guests do need somewhere to put cases, so either provide extra space in the wardrobe or a stand. The latter suits one-night people better as they don't unpack, not that some longer stay people do either. Whether you provide somewhere for cases or not, they will be stored on the floor, under the bed, or on top of the wardrobe. For bedside tables, the round chipboard ones will seem the cheapest, but by the time you've bought sets of circular cloths, plus either a washable one for the top or had a piece of glass cut, you could have bought a wood cabinet. The room will also need bedside mats if it isn't carpeted, and a full length mirror will always be appreciated.

armoire (f)	cupboard	lits superposés	bunk beds
cadre (m)	picture frame	literie (f)	bedding
chaise (f)	chair	matelas (m)	mattress
chevet (m)	bedside table	matelas en mousse	foam mattress
commode (m)	chest of drawers	matelas à ressorts	sprung mattress
descente de lit (f)	bedside mat	miroir (m)	mirror
dosseret (m)	bedhead	moquette (f)	fitted carpet
fauteuil (m)	arm chair	penderie (f)	wardrobe
lit (m)	bed	placard (m)	built in cupboard
lit à baldaquin	four poster	table (f)	table
lit de bébé	cot	table de toilette	dressing table
lit double	double bed	tablette (f)	shelf
lits jumeaux	twin beds	tableau (f)	picture
lit pliant	folding bed	tapis (m)	mat, rug
lit simple	single bed		

Figure 8   Bedroom furniture

Finishes

You'll have noticed that most hotels have carpet on the floor; it really is the quietest. And it is the easiest to keep clean provided it is a neutral colour with a slight texture. No need to buy the best quality. Boarding, whether old or new, always looks good but is noisy. The modern laminated wood flooring looks alright, though it doesn't fool anyone that it's genuine solid wood. But if poorly laid without enough expansion all round, it does not lie flat. Expansion is especially necessary at all doors. The cheaper quality is very susceptible to damp, and in the bedrooms damp can come from leaking radiators, overflowing en-suite bathrooms, windows left open, leaking roofs, frozen pipes, to name but a few. Tiles are suitable for the south and they can be laid on boarding with an underlay. For the walls it's paint or paper. If paint, there's the emulsion we know so well, there's a textured paint called *crépi*, or there's an expensive range called *Murs d'Autrefois* specially for the antique look. If you decide to paper, please go easy on the pattern. For the ceiling I wouldn't have anything other than white or the room looks gloomy.

Heating

The problem with heating guest bedrooms is they need to be to a living-room level of 19°C rather than a household bedroom level of 16°C. This is so that the room feels warm to walk into and because guests use it like a living-room to sit in. Which means it has to be heated for all those hours when they are out. When there aren't any guests booked, you could keep the heating on low and provide an electric fan heater if anyone turns up, though it's not ideal. You will obviously think hard about how many rooms to keep open in the winter.

Electricity

For general lighting, obviously you need a central pendant or wall brackets. For bedside lights, a pair of wall brackets is much better than bedside lamps as the latter do get broken. Guests also need a socket handy for recharging all their gadgets at your expense. The vacuum cleaner needs one anyway.

Themes

Some owners theme their rooms. I've heard of them being named after artists (French of course) with reproductions in the room, and that sounds interesting. I've seen others named after flowers or colours and that seems a bit ordinary. If it's a colour don't overdo it as I once heard an all-yellow bathroom described as looking like a bowl of custard. Numbering is easiest but it's a bit reminiscent of a hotel.

Finishing touches

It will not be expected that a B&B will have a room telephone and I'd be cautious about a TV because of sound transmission. If you have a mainly British clientele they will appreciate (or even expect) a tea-making facility; however, they do involve a lot of work and are likely to cause stains on walls, carpets, and bedspreads. They are not very common in France so it's not essential. Lastly, the room needs four door keys, one for the guests, one for the cleaner, one for when the guest goes home with theirs and does not post it back, and one for emergencies.

Now sleep in **each** of the bedrooms yourself for a week.

BATHROOMS

'Is there enough hot water?', asks Mrs Brit-with-the-cut-glass-accent on being shown her en-suite bathroom. Basil Fawlty would have had an answer to that, something like, 'Put another log on, Manuel. The lady needs a bath.'

The bathroom is so important now that I wonder if we shouldn't advertise 'bathroom with en-suite bedroom'. An en-suite bath or shower room is **essential** these days. 'H&C in all rooms' (euphemism for a washbasin) with the WC down the corridor just won't do any more. There's nothing for it but to provide a separate facility for each room, whatever it costs, which is a lot; and no cheating like putting a pre-fabricated shower cubicle in the corner. For the British baths reign supreme, but for other nationalities whether to have bath or shower rooms depends on the standard of your establishment and the available space. At grade four it needs to be bathrooms; at grade three it can be either.

The insertion of a bathroom into existing rooms needs careful planning, and I've seen examples where it's been badly done, in a situation where it could have been so much better. It's best to try and get as near the hotel standard plan as possible, *see Fig. 9*. If this can't be done then try and make it as unobtrusive as possible, *see Fig. 10*. A large square room needs an imaginative solution; *see Fig. 11* for an interesting idea. Bathrooms without a window can seem claustrophobic and dark in the daytime; a glazed door with a net curtain looks well and allows some light in.

I'm stating the obvious when I say that baths take a lot of hot water. It wouldn't be so bad if everyone didn't bathe at the same time, which is just before dinner. They've got the time and you are providing free hot water, aren't you? Save on the sanitary ware and have all white, but spend on the taps because they get hard use. Ease of cleaning is paramount and everything should be considered from that standpoint; there should be the minimum of exposed pipework.

Bath

Have a normal 170cm-long bath with a shower fitting. Don't go for oddities like a small size bath, an extra long one, or a jacuzzi. The latter are noisy

A STANDARD HOTEL BEDROOMS

Figure 9 Adding bathrooms

B SHOWER ROOMS ADDED
   TO EXISTING BEDROOMS

C BATHROOM ADDED TO
   LARGE EXISTING BEDROOM

Figure 10   *Figure 11*

and need explaining how to use. The best-looking screen to the bath/shower
is the single leaf glass frameless type. At grade 4 you will have to spend a lot
on the bathroom, and, if there's room, a free-standing bath looks very
trendy. In any case, the shower should be a separate fitting.

Basin

A basin set into a vanity top is much the easiest to keep clean, but don't
have a cabinet below. In fact don't have any cupboards in the bathroom:
too difficult to keep clean. Even a pedestal is a nuisance, have the basin

abattant (m)	WC seat	mélangeur (m)	mixer tap
beignoire (f)	bath tub	plan de toilette (m)	vanity top
cabine de douche (f)	shower cubicle	porte-serviettes (m)	towel rail
douche (f)	shower	receveur (m)	shower tray
lavabo (f)	basin	robinet (m)	tap
lave-mains (m)	hand-wash basin	WC (m)	WC

Figure 12 Bathroom fittings

on brackets if no vanity top. At grade 4 you should try and have two basins.

WC

If possible, have the suspended type with a concealed cistern, all in the interests of easy cleaning. Most are dual flush these days and you can get a silencing mechanism for most models (they're not all that silent). The French are still wary of the WC opening directly off the bedroom, or being situated in the bathroom, but the since the rest of the world accepts it, just keep the room smelling nice with a proprietary product. With a septic tank, some owners put notices up about restrictions. We didn't and were lucky enough never to have any trouble.

Bidet

I know France is the home of this article, but don't bother. The bum-washing function has now been taken over by the shower.

Shower

No one likes the smallest tray size of 75×75cm, so do have something larger. But, whatever you do, there's likely to be trouble when it's sited on a wooden floor. **Serious trouble**. Shower cubicles leak and do real damage to the house. The problem is likely to be hidden for a long time, until one day a portion of the floor or ceiling collapses. We tried curtains, folding doors, sliding doors, notices in several languages and still we had trouble. The worst offenders are unsupervised children. 'Oh I'm terribly sorry,' said a mother when we hammered on the door because water was pouring through the kitchen ceiling onto that night's dinner. She was sitting reading while her six-year-old showered without shutting the screen door. Some adults are not all that careful either. There's really no foolproof system for upstairs showers, but the best screens are glass in a metal frame. Plastic panels and frame can warp which means the doors don't close tightly. A downstairs shower with a tiled concrete floor can stand some water so you could have a walk-in cubicle with a fixed screen and no moving parts. There should be a thermostatic mixing valve, and since the flexible hoses have a very short life when used carelessly, you could consider building the fitting in.

Tiling

For the floor, have light-coloured tiles with dark joints. Light tiles don't show the dirt, and conversely dark joints don't show the dirt. I know you're going to be clean but no one's perfect. Laying the tiles diagonally looks good and conceals the fact of any walls not being at right angles. The cost of wall tiles varies enormously. Ignoring the institutional white, I would go for something moderately priced and then tile the whole room. Add a contrasting tiled dado line just above the basin and the room will look very smart. A final touch is to have the tiles above the dado a slightly lighter colour than the ones below.

Sundries

You need a towel rail or rack, mirror, glass shelf, waste bin, toilet-roll holder, soap dishes, somewhere for the spare toilet rolls, WC brush, tooth mug, something to hang the handwashed smalls on: in fact almost a trolley-full of items per bathroom from the DIY store. Note: a bin is **essential** or you could get nappies down the drain, with disastrous results. The bathroom lock should be of the type that is openable from the outside, as the last thing you need is a child locked in, though I realise that specialist ironmongery of this kind is only obtainable from builders' merchants. A window needs a roller blind or curtain or both.

People do need enough space to put all the toiletries/medecines/sponge bags they bring these days, so provide either enough shelf space or a decent vanity top. One dear soul arrived with 20 beauty products (yes, I did count, I couldn't resist it).

The elderly need some safety measures in the bathroom. Provide a stool and hand grips to the bath and shower. Could you also place a rubber safety mat somewhere discreet?

Disabled facility

Although a room can be specifically advertised for the disabled you may equally often want to use it for the able bodied. Shower rooms are a problem here because they will look institutional. Have coloured wall tiles and hang an attractive picture, and in the required space beside the WC put a small folding table with a lace cloth and a pretty pot plant.

KITCHEN

Breakfasts

An ordinary domestic kitchen is fine for breakfasts only. Or you could set up a mini kitchen in the actual dining room or a conservatory, and trolley the dirties to the dishwasher in the house kitchen. If you have an old house with a kitchen straight out of *Country Living* magazine, and only a couple of guest bedrooms, you could serve breakfasts there. You'd have to be super-tidy, unable to use it as a kitchen until they've finished eating and chatting, and accept that guests will invade it at any time of day because they will not regard it as private.

Dinners

This is a different matter. A lot will depend on the policy of your local inspector. If you do a lot of dinners they might be quite rigorous while in other areas they make no demands at all. In any case, a domestic kitchen is not really suitable, yet the scale of operations does not justify the big expense of a commercial installation. So the only thing to do is to get as near the commercial standard as possible. The room should be twice the area found in most modern houses, with a big central table.

A commercial kitchen has:
  – White wall tiles throughout
  – High level of fluorescent lighting
  – Glazed tile floor
  – All fittings and double sink/double drainer in stainless steel
  – Large gas cooker with extract hood
  – Open shelves for utensils and china
  – Walk-in larder for dry goods
  – Flat plastered ceiling
  – All fittings raised above floor level on legs to discourage vermin
  – Dishwasher

It would also help to have a walk-in cold store, but you'll need to have a big domestic larder-fridge and a chest freezer. Buy a cheap cooker just to get started but leave enough space for a larger one, and then later treat yourself to the monster you've always dreamed about – you deserve it! The normal

congélateur (m)	freezer	lave linge (m)	washing machine
évier (m)	sink	lave vaisselle (m)	dishwasher
frigo (m)	fridge	micro-onde (f)	microwave
four (m)	oven	plan de travail (m)	worktop
grille-pain (m)	toaster	plaque de cuisson (f)	hob top
hotte (f)	cooker hood	réfrigérateur (m)	refrigerator

Figure 13 Kitchen fittings

12-place 60cm-wide dishwasher will probably have to do, though actually they only just about cope with ten people and that's providing you don't put the pots and pans in. There are domestic machines available for 16 place settings at twice the price and they are 80cm wide. All commercial machines and cookers are very expensive. If you need a gas supply for the kitchen only, have the large double cylinders which are located outside. Worktops should be plastic, not tiled.

Safety

We had a fire extinguisher and fire blanket, even though these were not mandatory. Unfortunately a smoke detector sounds off at the first hint of burning toast, so it would have to be a heat detector if anything at all.

DINING ROOM

Setting the scene

To the French, the conviviality of the table is one of the essential ingredients of the menu. Therefore, as part of the family atmosphere, *chambres d'hôtes* are expected to have one large table. This doesn't always suit the insular British, so it had better be mentioned in your brochure. If the dining-room is a separate room you are lucky because it can laid or cleared at your leisure.

Furnishing

Finding a large enough table can be difficult and for more than eight it is extremely heavy (*see Fig. 14*). In fact it's so heavy that it's easy to make one that is indeed a fixture. Build a low wall near either end and have a joinery firm make a top. Or how about buying two and putting them together? This means they can be separated when there are only two people. The table must be big enough for **all** the guests at once. Even for breakfasts, they could all

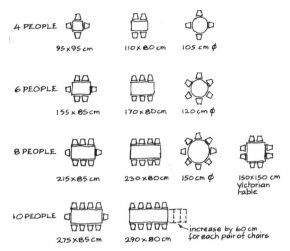

Figure 14 Dining table sizes

come down at once, especially if they are a group. Chairs should not be too heavy because the floor needs sweeping after every meal. There needs to be a sideboard for possibly putting some of the breakfast things on and for dishes and plates when serving dinner. Any other furnishings are for creating the right atmosphere.

Finishes

The French are untidy eaters – to our prim British eyes anyway – and the floor will be full of crumbs; it's even worse when there are babies. So **do not** have carpet. Tiles are much the best, and, for an old house, unglazed quarry tiles are the right choice. Ask at the DIY store for the correct treatment and cleaning method. It's not difficult, and it won't be long before they look as if they've always been there. Walls and ceiling should not be too dark, with

baby-foot (m)	table-football	fauteuil (m)	armchair
bibliothèque (f)	library	jeux de societé (m)	board/card games
billard (m)	billiard table	lampadaire (m)	standard lamp
buffet (m)	sideboard	plante d'apartement (f)	indoor plant
canapé (m)	sofa	poêle à bois (m)	wood-burning stove
chaise (f)	dining chair	table (f)	table
chaise de bébé	high chair	table ping-pong	table-tennis table
chaise roulante	wheel chair	télé (f)	TV
extincteur (m)	fire extinguisher		

Figure 15 Dining, lounge and games room furniture

finishes as for bedrooms. For a formal look to a plastered wall, have a dado rail at 90cm height with a darker colour below it.

LOUNGE

Traditionally all French life revolved around the big kitchen table, and in many homes this is still the custom; there is no living-room. Many French-run B&Bs still operate this way, so it's not necessarily expected that there will be one. In fact, if you're not doing dinners or your guests are all one-night stays, I wouldn't bother. But if you're offering the total holiday experience to an international clientele, then I'm sure you will have one.

Noise is always a problem. Holiday-makers like to stay up late and it may be necessary to remind them of children asleep upstairs. A bedroom opening directly off a lounge or dining room can also suffer here and really needs a lobby – just one square metre will be enough. If you happen to have provided a lounge a little out of the way or perhaps a north-facing room of no particular charm, it could turn out to be hardly ever used.

Furnishing
Comfortable sofas or armchairs should be provided for at least ⅔ of the guest capacity. The upholstery should have two sets of washable covers, and two-seater sofas are best because people don't like sitting three-in-a-row. Have some low tables that don't mind drinks being spilt on them. In addition, provide a table and chair for writing and a sideboard. Standard and table lamps can get broken; wall brackets are better. It is not difficult to collect enough paperbacks for a library, and guests do leave some behind (though do check them for pornography). We had to buy some second-hand French ones to keep the balance. A tiled or boarded floor with a loose mat that can be kept clear of the doors will last longer than a fitted carpet. One big indoor plant, say a ficus, makes an impact on the room, whereas small plants on the window sill just make work.

Heating
An open log fire or a stove will prove irresistible, but the room needs conventional heating as well. However, all this is expensive and you may

consider closing the room when there are few guests in the winter. Instead, make some space in the dining-room which has to be heated anyway, and just have the minimum of a couple of armchairs.

Television

There is no solution to suit everyone. The British are greater addicts than the French, and other nationalities are not much interested in either country's transmissions. There are four possibilities:

1. No TV, especially if already provided in the bedrooms.

2. Only have French television.

3. Your own country's TV via satellite since you will have targeted clients from that country. There is an hour's time difference to the UK, so it does make the popular programmes rather late.

4. Go for as many channels as possible and let the guests sort it out for themselves.

For the record, we had French TV only; we felt that if we had British as well, then they would hog it. So actually it wasn't used much, and those who did express an opinion said they didn't need to watch on holiday. If you want satellite programmes for yourselves, the dish would have to be hidden from the guests' view or they will feel hard done by. Even if you haven't room for a large lounge, you could have a small TV room, or it could go in a games room with the implication that it's for children. Everyone will want to watch the World Cup and then it doesn't matter what language the commentary is. Have a basic remote control zapper that only changes the channels. This stops a too-clever 11-year-old improving the settings.

British sets work on the PAL system and receive British TV only via a satellite dish unless you are near the Channel. To register for reception, you have to provide a UK address. French TV uses the SECAM system, but all sets are now dual standard. It is illegal to show videos to paying guests because there is a copyright fee, though occasionally guests bring their own.

GAMES ROOM

A fitted-out room is expensive and only worth it if you have the maximum number of bedrooms and long-staying guests. There is the cost of renovating the room, the weekly cost of lighting and cleaning, and the annual cost of upkeep and maintenance. It will be well used provided it is not too isolated. If the area is an outbuilding a bit separated from the house, it would be better opened up to the outside and considered as an adjunct to outdoor living. Table-tennis is quite cheap to provide with an indoor table costing about £100 but remember it needs a high ceiling. Billiards is popular but a table is expensive and very heavy, so it needs a solid floor. Table-football and darts are popular too. Provide some board games and playing cards either here or in the lounge. Scrabble is the most popular and you need a French set as it's slightly different. You can also set chess pieces out on a board on a side table to encourage people to play, or have a jig-saw puzzle permanently on the go. There should be a table and chairs for playing: plastic garden furniture will do very well.

HALL

The room that visitors enter first needs to sparkle. A large display of fresh flowers is the best, but only if you have time to look after it. Otherwise, have some mirrors or brassware or a big floor-standing pot of artificial flowers (nothing twee, mind). A few B&Bs have a reception desk and a presentable one can be made from a sideboard with the back removed. But some branches of *Gîtes de France* veto this as being too much like a hotel. There must be a table or some other top for putting out the tourist information, or it could alternatively go in the lounge or dining-room. Also, the international clientele needs a good French/English dictionary handy to help the conversations along. A payphone should be here if you have one, and just inside the front door is the place for a fire extinguisher.

If your establishment caters for sports persons or hikers, they will come in with plenty of dirty boots and other equipment. Could they be relegated to a side entrance and lobby just for them?

If possible provide a downstairs toilet for casual visitors, for anyone working for you, and for elderly guests who find stairs difficult. The stairs should be well lit and ideally have a firm handrail both sides.

GUESTS' KITCHEN

If you don't do dinners this is a good idea, but no hotel has a kitchen for guests; they are supposed to patronise the restaurant. When you do provide a kitchen, it needs at least a small cooker, sink, microwave, and fridge-freezer. Have open shelves rather than cabinets for ease of cleaning and provide the usual crockery, utensils and cleaning materials. You could have a dishwasher, but in any case this is one place where there will have to be notices about leaving the room clean for others. Since the area needs table and chairs, this kitchen could be a corner of the dining-room used for breakfasts.

If there's not room for a full kitchen, how about one of the mini-kitchens available? They come as a complete unit with everything necessary except the plumbing and electricity supply. They are about 1m wide × 60cm deep, depending on the model, and that's about the size of a wardrobe.

Any provision for guests to prepare their own food or drink makes for a lot of cleaning. If there isn't a kitchen, a fridge for the guests is usually appreciated. They will often take picnic lunches and will prefer to store their favourite cold drinks. It could be in a corridor or in the lounge and these are available in brown which looks better.

STORAGE

There is never enough. A **large** linen cupboard is essential. Multiply a domestic cupboard by three to get an idea of the size required for half a dozen bedrooms. There should be a cleaning cupboard on each floor, and a general store somewhere on the ground floor. The size of this store will determine how much you can buy in bulk. All stores should be locked.

UTILITY ROOM

There is so much washing in a B&B that it's a real nuisance in the kitchen and generally a separate room with a washing machine, dryer and sink is ideal. It doesn't even have to be in the house, but if this is the case do watch out for freezing weather. In reality a B&B requires more capacity than that supplied by a domestic machine, commercial ones are much too expensive so plump for two ordinary machines. These will be cheaper and will give useful back up for break downs.

OFFICE

Where will you have the nerve centre for this whole enterprise? It only consists of a desk big enough for the computer and telephone, a filing cabinet and a stationery cupboard. But it needs to be somewhere to work quietly, yet be able to keep an eye on most of what is going on. Somewhere off the hall or the kitchen are the usual choices for a larger business; for the smaller establishment a desk in your own living-room would suffice, but remember there will be a lot of telephone calls.

STAFF QUARTERS

That is: yourselves. If the guests are in another building, then there's no privacy problem indoors, only in the garden. If the guests share the house with you, it depends how self-contained you want to be. If there are more than three bedrooms, you will probably find that number of people intrusive and really need separate accommodation. The ideal is a wing of the house for yourselves with the kitchen common to both. It is not difficult to add a stair between a downstairs sitting-room and a bedroom or two upstairs. With an outside door this will make you totally self-contained, and is easily heated if the rest of the house is closed. That's all very well for a rambling farm house; a tall town house is more difficult. You could end up with your sitting-room on the lower ground floor (euphemism for basement), and your bedroom on the second floor. I hope you thought ahead when buying the property and can manage better than this. There may be a need for a bedroom for an employee in the summer and then a room in the attic may have to suffice, provided there are some toilet facilities.

TIPS FOR MAKING IT PAY

◆ Have good beds.
◆ Have good bathrooms.
◆ Do not have single rooms.
◆ Do not have too many ornaments.

TIP FOR IMPROVING YOUR FRENCH

◆ Watch the television news in French.

6

Barns and Outside

If you're looking for a property in the centre of a village, and since many are built on hillsides, it should be possible to find one with a view from the back of the building. If there's space enough for a terrace this can be ideal. No garden to look after, a terrace for serving breakfasts and sitting out in the evening (even though you don't do dinners) and a manageable house. (In the best scenario the back of the house and any terrace should both face west.)

The trouble here is that many Brits look at rural France with its sparse population and are seduced by the large tracts of land our money will buy, without realising the enormous amount of labour needed to look after such acres.

SMALL OUTBUILDINGS

These are fairly easy to convert to bedrooms and should be within the scope of DIY. They need to be well done so that people don't feel they are being fobbed off, though however hard you try, they may still refer to being 'in the annex', which is slightly derogatory. If you give them their own front door and a covered terrace with garden furniture, this will make amends. When the buildings round a farm courtyard are attractively converted, the whole ensemble can look delightful. Heating and hot water are a problem with scattered buildings; you'll probably need individual electric heaters. If there are several rooms, all large enough to contain a couple of armchairs and a TV, then they are self-contained and no one need come into the house except for meals.

LARGE BARNS

Either way: you live in the barn and put the B&B in the house, or you live in the house and put the B&B in the barn – this is major construction and you need professional help. Most importantly, the barn conversion needs a carefully considered plan because, in essence, they are not very suitable for humans; they were built for animals. They have many disadvantages:

◆ They are wide and have a high roof ridge, so how are you going to provide light in the centre and what will you do with all that roof space?

◆ They were invariably part full height and part two-storey, with the ground floor of the two-storey part having a very low ceiling, just enough for cows.

◆ Both the upper and lower floor levels usually slope; that's to help the mucking out.

◆ The windows are small because they are for ventilation not for looking out.

◆ One enormous opening for farm machinery.

◆ The construction is not of the same standard as a house.

The latter is the most serious problem. Even if the old timbers are still sound, they may need strengthening or renewing; and any new load-bearing walls and posts inside will need new foundations. To tell the truth, I have never seen a really well-planned conversion of a large barn into a B&B, but I'm sure that in expert hands it can be done. The cost will be more than putting up a wholly new building. Allow **at least** a year for the actual building work even if you entrust it completely to a general contractor. If you want to organise any of it or even do some of the work yourself, better allow twice that. However at the end of the day you should have a building with a lot of character, which is what we all want for our B&B.

PARKING

If you're in a village and you haven't any on-site parking, it must be mentioned in the brochure. You will lose some custom because visitors are often carrying a lot of luggage and are loath to unload just for one night.

If you have the land, you need a gravelled parking place for each bedroom plus one or two spare. Grass won't do as it soon gets muddy. Shade is a priority so you could plant some trees, which probably won't acquire a useful size during your tenure of the property. Under cover in a barn is superb, but I really think a barn should be put to a more profitable use. Some cover is required for bicycles and motor bikes. If the parking is away from the house, people will still want to come to the front door to unload. I would have a notice about not taking responsibility for parked cars.

GARDEN

In some *départements* Gîtes de France have created a guide specially for houses with beautiful gardens (called *Gîte au Jardin*) but unless you're keen enough to reach this standard don't knock yourself out trying to create an English garden – the climate in France is somewhat different. In most of the country it's not that the annual rainfall is low, it's that two month's worth comes all at once in a ten-minute storm. So for most of the summer the ground is baked dry and you'd find automatic sprinklers very expensive; in fact they're banned if there's a drought. Window-boxes in towns and plants in pots everywhere are the thing. Geraniums in summer and pansies in winter are the usual choices, but there's nothing to stop you being more individual. Hanging baskets need watering **three times a day** in very hot weather.

To find out what does succeed in a different climate and soil, look around at what is flourishing in everyone else's garden. The climate in the south is too dry for flower beds which would need watering every day, and all water is metered. Have some water butts to catch all that storm water. Shrubs are fine, but both they and trees need watering frequently for the first two years. If you have a large area, don't skimp on the ride-on mower. For about an acre a small model will do, but more than that needs a big machine – preferably with all the add-ons. Have some tables and chairs in shady spots and they will be much appreciated for picnic lunches. Then you need somewhere discreet for all the washing lines, and if there is a continuing programme of building work, it needs an area to store the mixer and materials. The entrance to the property **must** give a good first impression, so keep the path weeded and the geraniums fertilized, but otherwise reduce the gardening to what you have time for. If any areas can't be maintained, either let them go wild or grass the whole lot.

TERRACE

A paved terrace for outdoor breakfast and dinners is a great asset. The area can be gravel but paving looks better. If some of the area is covered, it can be used in the middle of the day as well, otherwise it will be too hot. Carrying the meals out of doors does make more work, but the guests love it. Provide a barbecue and lighting, together with a large table and chairs, and you have an outside room that will be used a lot.

SWIMMING POOL

Why a pool

If you're in the south and not near the sea, and you're aiming at the holiday trade, then a pool is **essential.** Even if you are near a public pool or a lake with swimming facilities, I would still have your own. The only exceptions I would make are in the mountains because walking will give quite enough exercise, and altering the contours of a mountainside for a pool is expensive; and on a working farm. But for a clientele that is merely passing through, then a pool is a luxury extra; it will increase the business a little of course. A standard 12m × 6m pool, with basic accessories, paving, winter cover, landscaping and safety fencing, will cost about £25,000 and about £5,000 for solar heating.

Siting

This is crucial to the enjoyment of such an expensive facility. If near the house, it looks good in the photographs, but a pool is noisy and if you stay open in the winter it will have to remain uncovered and you'll have to continue with the cleaning. A pool with its winter cover on does not look good, but keeping it uncovered is not entirely wasted effort as people do like to sit in the sunshine even when they have no intention of going in. The noise is not only children; there are late night revellers too.

A pool sited apart from the house keeps the noise away, and it can be covered in the winter. The disadvantages are that it will need extensive landscaping and, apart from aerial photos, it can't appear in the same picture as the house. This is annoying because many guide books allow only one photo. Ideally a pool should be sited on flat land to avoid the expense of retaining walls, but this is seldom possible. In any location it **must** be sheltered and away from trees.

Construction

Rectangular pool sizes: up to three bedrooms 10×5 metres

          four to six bedrooms 12×6 metres

          with other facilities 14×7 metres or larger

Prefabricated pools only go up to 9-metre length, but are the least expensive.

Most pools of 10×5m or larger are built on site with a concrete base, blockwork sides rendered, and with a plastic liner. They can be any shape or size (*see Fig. 16*).

There is also a patented system using corrugated steel sides, with a sand base and plastic liner, see 'Waterair' under Addresses. Good for curved shapes.

All pools have pre-cast concrete edging with paving or timber slats. Don't have gravel around the pool. Apart from being hard on the feet, you will find it being thrown into the water by children. Most pools have Roman steps, and sometimes a ladder as well. Ladders are not good for children. The usual depth is 1m at the shallow end and 2.4m at the deep end. This is

Figure 16 Swimming pools

not deep enough for diving, thank goodness. The filtration system can be either chlorine or salt based; the latter is much preferred by the guests. A salt system costs more to install, but it is cheaper in the long run because othewise a pool needs a lot of chlorine but only a little salt each year. There are computer controlled filter systems which will save a lot of time and give a better result. The prefabricated pools do not need lining but other pools do, and there is a choice here between plastic liners (the cheapest option) or painting or tiling (the most expensive option). A liner should last ten years, more if you patch it, but painting needs frequent renewing, and tiling must be expertly done if it is to be trouble-free. A lined plastic pool must not be emptied or the liner will collapse.

Extras

Don't go over the top, but a few little luxuries can surely be included in the budget. A couple of underwater lights don't cost much and it looks good in the brochure to say 'floodlit pool'. A solar shower is great fun and saves most of the sun tan oil accumulating in the water and leaving a greasy mark. The shower needs a tiled tray. Don't try and manage without a proper winter cover. An ordinary tarpaulin will lift off in the wind no matter how hard you try and weight it down. Without any cover or maintenance at all through the winter, the pool will be a dirty green soup by the spring and an enormous job to clean. Provide plenty of sun loungers and umbrellas, don't make people fight for them. They don't last long and some must be replaced every year.

Water temperature

Only the hardy will swim in a temperature below 22°C; the keen will use the pool between 22° and 24°, and the rest of humanity likes 24° at least. In most of France you should reach 22° minimum between mid June and mid September with 24°–26° for most of July and August, but it depends on location and elevation. A night-time cover is essential if the pool is heated, but even without heating this will increase the temperature by 3°; they are a chore to take on and off and, like most things these days, can be electrically operated. Perhaps the enthusiasts who want to swim before breakfast can be persuaded to take it off themselves. I am convinced that heating the water is the **next big thing** and I recommend you think seriously about it, preferably before building the pool. More and more people have it and you could be losing out to the competition otherwise. Solar panels can be either on a roof or on the ground, but many are needed and they do look ugly. Alternatives are a heat pump, or even a conventional boiler. You need to get quotes for the various systems. Naturally, heating is more of an asset in the north; in the south it should increase the swimming season by a month each end, but that is when there aren't so many guests around. It needs careful consideration.

Pool house

The minimum provision is a housing for the machinery, either in an existing building or something specially built. Since people also need somewhere shady to lounge, could a barn be converted? An open-sided tent makes a pleasant place to sit, but when left up permanently it is susceptible to damage by summer storms. A real asset would be a WC by the pool; if you don't provide one where are the children to 'go'? (don't tell me).

The contractor

A large pool is beyond the scope of DIY. Get three quotes from experienced installers in the area. They will advise on the siting, get the necessary permissions, and give a ten-year guarantee on the construction. Allow at least three months for the building, and keep chivvying the builder or it will never get done in time. Constructing a pool makes an enormous disruption of the garden: be prepared. If the soil from digging the hole can be distributed on your land it will be much cheaper than taking it away, but there is a lot of it. There will be a hefty water bill in the following January.

Cleaning

Allow ½ an hour a day, seven days a week when the pool is in use. You need an automatic vacuum cleaner plus skimmer and brushes. Take the winter cover off in mid-April to give a fortnight or more for a thorough clean, and it should be ready for use by 1st May.

Safety

The recent law which required all pools to have a safety certificate by 2006 has caused much anguish. It is designed to protect children under five and is intended to supplement supervision, not to supplant it. Whether this will be achieved remains to be seen. The regulations have been added to the *Code de la Construction et de l'Habitation* (Building Regulations) and are not available to the public because they are intended to be implemented by professionals. You won't get insurance without the certificate. Briefly the requirements are:

◆ Certified barriers and gates (which I regret to say are not pretty). These can be combined with unclimbable walls at least 1.1m high. (These could be retaining walls and all walls provide shelter and reflect warmth.)

◆ A certified alarm system. (Check that your robot cleaner is compatible.)

◆ A certified, stout, lockable cover or shelter.

◆ Any custom or home made system certified by an approved specialist. The cost would be €500–€600 and you can contact the official body *Afnor* for advice in English.

Even with all the safety precautions you can think of, a pool is still a big worry. We had a 14-year-old dive into the shallow end and hit her head on the bottom, and a pregnant woman slipped on the steps. Fortunately neither came to any serious harm.

Other types of pool

What do I think of above ground pools? I think they look like you can't afford a proper one. At the other end of the scale designer pools look fabulous, but the sky's the limit on cost and they can't be paid for by the profit from a B&B.

But here's another idea for something different to the standard choices yet is still reasonably affordable – an ecologic pool. Generally known as a bio pool, they use natural methods of filtration, are easy to clean and are a delight to look at in all seasons. The cost is comparable to a standard one of the same size. Several have been installed in *chambres d'hôtes* and a visit would be helpful. Go to www.bioteich.com for more information.

GROW YOUR OWN

If you do dinners, this is a lovely idea for those who have the land, the time, and the enthusiasm. As well as vegetables you should consider growing flowers for cutting, a great saving on the petty cash. If you've not got that sort of time, how about an orchard, though trees need five to ten years before they produce much? If nothing else, at least grow your own herbs.

There are tax advantages if you can persuade the powers that be that you are an agricultural business and the B&B is a sideline. It's a matter of the area you have under cultivation that counts and this is not so large, so consult your *Chambre d'Agriculture* if you think you might qualify. You even get a larger grant for converting the rooms for the B&B.

ANIMALS

These are absolute winners if you feel up to it. I don't mean domestic pets. In order of expense I mean donkeys, llamas, pot bellied pig, rabbits or birds in cages, fantail pigeons, ducks, fish in a tank. I'm told that chickens are almost a paying proposition, provided a fox or pack of dogs doesn't get them. Almost any animal gives the establishment a rural atmosphere.

BOULES COURT

This comes before a swimming pool; it's certainly a lot cheaper. It has to be absolutely flat, and is constructed of hardcore, clinker, and a topping of limestone and sharp sand, all firmly compacted with a mechanical roller. It should have an edging and old railway sleepers look better than concrete. Size 20–27.5 metres long × 2.5–4 metres wide.

CHILDREN'S AREA

A swing is the obvious first item, or perhaps a whole play apparatus with climbing rope, slide, etc. The posts must be set in concrete and the climbing ropes should be checked regularly. However, some people consider that swings are dangerous, and a simple log for balancing on or a climbing frame is better. **Do not** have a sand pit; it will be a lavatory for all the neighbourhood cats. To keep little children away from the main pool, you could have an inflatable plastic paddling pool just in high season.

OTHER LEISURE ACTIVITIES

Do not provide more than you can find the time to maintain properly. Broken equipment looks bad. Badminton is cheap because it is played on grass. An outdoor table-tennis table is popular and it will be used even more if it can be under cover – say, in an open barn. There's clock golf, croquet, and outdoor chess. There is even a B&B where the proprietor laid out four holes of golf and found it very popular, or you could have a practise net. Renting out bicycles is profitable if you know how to maintain them; hirers don't mend their own punctures. You may prefer to save on the administration and include bicycles in the free facilities.

If you fancy something outrageously expensive like a tennis court, an indoor swimming pool or a squash court, then now is your chance to put it down as a business expense. But it really must be for your own pleasure; it cannot be justified commercially for a B&B.

WOODLAND AND HEDGES

Even woodland needs maintaining. The undergrowth needs clearing and dying trees need felling otherwise they are dangerous. If the undergrowth is not dealt with, the wood will be impenetrable after five years. There are government grants for planting trees; ask at the *Chambre d'Agriculture*.

Cutting your own trees for firewood is a nice idea; oak is by far the best. Don't try and cut down a tree yourself. It takes experience to know which way it is going to fall. The usual arrangement for someone else cutting them is that if they take half the logs, the work will be done at no cost. Logs are bought in one-metre lengths, so, for all but the largest open fires, they need cutting. You will need a chain saw or electric log cutter. Logs should be stored under cover or under a tarpaulin. For seasoning two years will do, but five years are better.

There is also government help for planting hedges in the countryside. They will be mixed native species, and provided there is at least a 100-metre run they don't have to be between fields. The plants, stakes and plastic ground cover are provided at a very low cost, then you either plant the hedge yourself or help can be given, but that has to be paid for. Ask at the *Chambre d'Agriculture*.

YET MORE LAND

With land so much cheaper, you may now own more than you ever dreamed possible. If it's already let for agricultural use, then it's practically impossible to break the lease. Rents are very low and you'll be lucky to pocket a few hundred pounds. This means that you should not accept money for letting anyone use your land for any form of agriculture, or you could create a lease which will be hard to get out of. What is to be done with it? It shouldn't just be left to grow weeds. The obvious first option is to enlarge the garden and plant ornamental trees. Another idea is to let a farmer take the hay for his animals, perhaps in return for some goat's cheese? For major garden alterations it really is best to call in help with the right machinery. Trying to shift earth or clear large areas by hand is not practical.

EXTRA ACCOMMODATION

With all the bedrooms in the house in use it's tempting to look at all the land you own to provide space for more. For example, you could site a caravan very discreetly for the residential help in the summer; do however ask at the *marie* for information because there are strict rules. Guests will probably accept it as a temporary expedient, but on the whole it doesn't look good.

For an extra guest room how about a tree house? They're a wow with children and I don't mean the kind for playing in, I mean one with a real bedroom and shower room. These are expensive of course because of the short season. Except in the case of very large trees, the tree house is supported on pilotis on the ground so there is no weight resting on the tree itself. It would need to be properly constructed by an expert (go to www.la-cabane-perchee.com for more info).

SEPTIC TANK

You need to use an activator (as sold in supermarkets) regularly in the season and if the premises have been empty for a period. Also use some if a quantity of bleach or a caustic drain clearing product has been used. There will be a grease trap outside the kitchen, and this needs clearing at least once a year. The main tank should be emptied every four years. If a septic tank smells, and it has not been overloaded, then there is something wrong and it should be looked at by a specialist.

RUBBISH

This is one dirty big problem because there is so much of it. If doing dinners, you need one domestic-size bin for each bedroom plus one for yourselves. I hope there is a collection in your area, but even then you have to take it to the roadside. If there is no collection, then you are faced with taking it to the nearest public bin. In this case you could ask at the town hall if there is a commercial arrangement. Bottle banks have existed for many years and you will collect a great many, so you need to provide some containers. More and more communes now expect you to sort the rubbish into various re-cyclable categories and, with the quantities produced, you will find this a real chore. The enclosure should be kept clean to avoid insects; should not have food

arbre (m)	tree	ordure (f)	rubbish
arbuste (m)	shrub	parc (m)	estate
arroser	to water	parking (m)	car park
arrosoir (m)	watering can	paysagiste (m)	landscape gardener
badminton (m)	badminton	pergola (f)	pergola
bain de soleil (m)	sun lounger	piscine (f)	swimming pool
balançoire (f)	garden swing	plante (f)	plant
bois (m)	woodland	plante grimpante	climbing plant
boulodrome (m)	boules court	plate-bande (f)	flower bed
brouette (f)	wheelbarrow	portail (m)	entrance gate
bulbe (m)	bulb	portique (m)	play equipment
champ (m)	field	potager (m)	vegetable garden
clôture (f)	fence	poubelle (f)	rubbish bin
court (m)	tennis court	prairie (f)	meadow
déchetterie (f)	public tip	remorque (f)	car trailer
dépendence (f)	outbuilding	salon de jardin (f)	garden furniture
engrais (m)	fertilizer	store (m)	awning
fleur (f)	flower	terrain (m)	land
gazon (m)	lawn	terrasse (f)	terrace
grange (f)	barn	terreau (m)	compost
graine (f)	seed	tondeuse (f)	lawn mower
gravier (m)	gravel	tondeuse auto-portée	ride on mower
haie (f)	hedge	tri (m)	sorting of rubbish
herbe (f)	grass	vélo (m)	bicycle
jardin (m)	garden	vélo tout terrain (VTT)	mountain bike
jardinier (m)	gardener	verger (m)	orchard
mauvaise herbe (f)	weed		

Figure 17   Glossary

left in loose bags to attract rats; and should be dog proof to avoid rubbish spread all over the garden one day. There will always be a public tip in your area which you are entitled to use for large items.

TIPS FOR MAKING IT PAY

◆ In the country have a pool to encourage long-stay visitors.
◆ Have a terrace for outdoor meals.
◆ Don't try and make an English garden.
◆ Have a variety of outdoor occupations.

TIP FOR IMPROVING YOUR FRENCH

◆ Read a French magazine such as *Paris Match* or *Le Nouvel Observateur*.

7

The Table

BREAKFAST

The terms of your drinks licence will be such that even non-alcoholic drinks can only be served to resident guests with a meal. So it should always be mentioned in your publicity that the price includes breakfast. Of course it will be a continental breakfast, but that's not the apology for a 'full English' that you get in UK hotels when they want to fob us off with something cheaper. Admittedly the 'full continental' doesn't include a cooked course but it is plentiful. At the absolute minimum it includes: several types of bread, jams, croissants or similar pastries, orange juice and a choice of hot beverage. For a better spread it can have: yoghurt, cereals, fruit salad, fresh fruit, cake, the option of boiled eggs, and even the selection of cold meat and cheese that is more northern European than French. It really depends on how much you charge for B&B.

Time

A few proprietors have one fixed time for breakfast and this is not liked. We said between 7.45 and 10.00 which seemed OK. Occasionally people wanted to make an earlier start and then we left them something.

Beverage

We offered orange juice plus a choice of tea, coffee, decaffeinated coffee, hot chocolate and herb tea. Buy good quality cartons of 100 per cent pure orange juice. Better still, press it from fresh oranges as most people drink it for their health. Over 60 per cent of the vitamin C content is lost during the packaging process and more still if cartons are left open. The French like their tea weak by our standard and without milk (they believe strong tea is bad for the nerves), so always provide a jug of hot water. The coffee should be freshly percolated: either give a fresh pot to people as they arrive or have insulated jugs. Children like hot chocolate; a few adults do too, so you'll have to learn how to make it and it is served in large cups. For herb tea *verveine* (verbena) is the most popular. Fresh milk is hard to come by every day so we used long life. Note that granulated sugar is for cooking; lump sugar is for the table.

Bread, pastries and cake

Everyone has the mental picture of crusty bread and buttery croissants – a dream that is becoming ever harder to fulfil as small bakers are closing by the hundred every year. We did collect fresh bread by car every morning, but the shop wasn't open every day in winter and it's a chore when there are only two guests. When fresh bread wasn't available it's best to freeze the *pain de campagne* (country loaf), then de-frost it in a microwave, sprinkle with water, and pop it in a hot oven for 10 minutes. An alternative is to buy the part-baked bread, but this is expensive. Or you could bake your own in one of those machines, but that's also expensive and it doesn't make a French-shaped loaf.

Always buy good butter croissants; the large supermarket packs are poor. Croissants can also be frozen and freshened up in the oven, though of course it's not quite so good. As an alternative, you can have *pain au raisin* (Chelsea buns), and children like *pain au chocolat*. As well as ordinary bread, put out some *brioche* (a light milk bread), and either *biscottes* or *pains grillés* (both these are pre-toasted bread). Lean heavily on your baker for an account and a 10 per cent discount; you'll be buying a lot. The French prefer their butter unsalted.

For a French breakfast, think 'tea time' because they really do have bread and butter and jam, and cake. Well, only occasionally cake, and by *'cake'* they mean 'fruit cake'. Home-made is wonderful only if you've got the time, which I didn't have, as I tried it once and it wasn't popular with other nationalities.

Jam

But I did make all the jam. Really it's not that difficult, but you need a lot. One trouble is that many fruits ripen in high season, and some of the taste is lost if they are frozen for making up later. Honey is popular too, but the French do not like the English-style chunky marmalade, so it wasn't always put out.

Plum is the cheapest jam to make; strawberry and apricot are the most popular. These fruits can be bought in bulk in the market. Quince jelly will be new to many and sounds very rural. The British staple of blackberry and apple is not possible due the lack of blackberries (not enough rain) and lack of suitable apples (they don't have Bramleys). *Oranges amères* (Seville oranges) for marmalade are only available in the larger markets. Use ordinary granulated sugar, except for strawberries which must either have the special jam-making sugar or a setting agent. Many French still make their own jam and the big preserving pans are widely available. The country folk have a gas ring in an outhouse for making preserves. You could do the same and make vast quantities and sell some to the guests – you'll have to judge whether it really is profitable. Use the paraffin wax sold for food use for sealing the jars and you'll never be bothered with ants.

It looks generous to put four varieties of home-made jam on the table, and when one day a man came into the kitchen to compliment me on my apricot jam, it made the all effort seem worthwhile.

Other points

The glossary (*Fig. 18*) contains the basics for a continental breakfast. Yoghurt should be good quality, and **do not** have the hotel-type butters and jams in little packs.

assiette (f)	plate	maison	home-made
beurre (m)	butter	nappe (f)	tablecloth
beurre doux	unsalted butter	œuf (m)	egg
boulangerie (f)	bakery	œuf en coque	hard boiled egg
café (m)	coffee	pain (m)	bread
café décaféiné	decafinated coffee	pain de compagne	country bread
café soluble	instant coffee	pain au raisin	Chelsea bun
cafetière (f)	coffee pot	petit-déjeuner (m)	breakfast
cake (m)	fruit cake	petit pain (m)	bread roll
chocolat (m)	drinking chocolate	pichet (m)	jug
confiture (f)	jam, marmalade	porcelaine (f)	china
couteau (m)	knife	serviette (f)	napkin
cuillère (f)	spoon	soucoupe (f)	saucer
cuillère à café	tea spoon	sucre (m)	sugar
jus d'orange (m)	orange juice	sucre en morceaux	lump sugar
lait (m)	milk	sucrier (m)	sugar bowl
lait demi-écrémé	semi-skimmed milk	tasse (f)	cup
lait écrémé	skimmed milk	thé (m)	tea
lait entier	full cream milk	théière (f)	teapot
lait frais	fresh milk	tisane (f)	herb tea
lait UHT	long life milk	yaourt (m)	yoghurt

Figure 18 Glossary for breakfasts

Laying on a copious breakfast means that a few people will squirrel away something for their lunch. They think they are getting something for nothing. They aren't. In fact it's the other way round; you are benefiting from their warm feeling for the few cents cost of an apple. So go all out to encourage it.

TABLE D'HOTE

The words *table d'hôte* have no exact translation into English. The Larousse dictionary defines it as: *table servie à heures fixes et à tant par tête* (meals served at fixed hours at so much per head), which seems a fair description. But it's difficult for us foreigners to know quite what standard to aim for. The answer is that it should be good home cooking, such as you would serve to friends and family on a slightly formal occasion. Bear in mind that in France this means a convivial meal of at least four courses with wine, but it need not be as formal as a good restaurant.

Offering dinners is a very big decision because it is so much work. We didn't have a *table d'hôte* for the first three years, then when we added it the business increased greatly. Many people will only stay where they can have dinner, so you get more clients for the B&B as well as the profit on the meals. If you're in a village with a couple of restaurants within walking distance, there's no imperative to do dinners. In the country with no restaurant near then you will have to do dinners. It is reckoned that a *table d'hôte* increases the occupancy by at least 20 nights a year and it doubles the income per room, **but** that it can take up as much as 50 per cent of your time. Think carefully about the commitment.

The reasons for eating at a *table d'hôte* are:

◆ Reluctance to go out again after a long journey.
◆ Liking a drink with the meal.
◆ Not wanting to take children to a restaurant.
◆ Wanting to put children to bed at a reasonable hour.
◆ Looking forward to the good cooking promised in the brochure.

Though keen cooks, neither of us had any commercial experience, and we did find the dinners very hard work. From mid-June to mid-September we were doing four to twelve dinners a day, seven days a week, with only a handful of days in about 14 weeks when no-one wanted to eat in. It wasn't possible to take turns either, as it takes two to cook, serve and clear up. I hope I've not painted too daunting a picture; there are ways to lighten the load, and there were rewards apart from the obvious one that it's profitable. Notwithstanding their anti-British prejudice we found that the French eat in more than the other nationalities. After all, the local restaurants are no novelty for them and they are suspicious of eating where they have no reliable recommendation. The sound of a table full of guests all chatting away, sometimes in two or even three languages, was very gratifying. And the compliments received made it seem very worthwhile.

PROFIT

A hotelier told me that a restaurant price should consist of one third the cost of the ingredients, one third overheads, and one third profit. Hmm . . . I don't think we came near this with such small numbers. We found about ⅔ of our guests had dinner, but this varies a lot between establishments. We found that even people in our *gîte* had dinner occasionally. Out of season we were often doing a meal for two and that doesn't pay unless the price is very high; we reckoned it needed six to see much of a profit. A *table d'hôte* has a **fixed price** and does not have a choice of menus, but you may offer a gourmet meal at an increased price. Look through the brochures and see what other people are charging. You will find it's a lot less than restaurant prices in the UK.

LIGHTEN THE LOAD

There are a few possibilities. The first is to hire help for the evenings, but it would have to be a flexible arrangement because, even in high season, the number at the table can vary from none to a full house. The duties would be to lay the table, serve, clear away, load the dishwasher, wash up and tidy the kitchen, sweep the dining-room floor and lay the breakfast. At least then the chef could leave off work as soon as the main course is served. You need to pay only a little over the minimum wage for this, but if you hire someone to do the actual cooking they will want more.

Another way is not to serve dinner every day. Check that the local restaurants aren't closing the same day. There are several disadvantages to this. Firstly, once your customers have eaten out, they may continue to do so, and you lose business. Secondly, you have got to warn people when they book, because they never read the brochure closely. And lastly, it is difficult to have a demi-pension reduction.

Alternatively you could only do dinners in high season when there will be a full table. At the opposite end of the scale is the host with only one or two bedrooms who offers dinner only on the day of arrival; if you regularly invite some friends as well it could be fun, though you won't make much.

If you don't do dinners at all, how about negotiating with a restaurant for a 10 per cent off voucher for your guests' first night? Most establishments would go along with this. You'd have to mention it in your brochure and make some arrangements for booking.

DEMI-PENSION

It is expected that there will be a reduction for stays of a few days with dinners. *Gîtes de France* recommend three days, but five or seven days are also common. You don't have to, and it makes for problems, mainly in that it commits you to cooking every single day. If you do want to take one day a week off, or go to some special event, what will you charge if a meal is not available? Or you'll have to make some alternative arrangements. Nevertheless, demi-pension does help to fill the table, and if you want to make money doing meals, you have got to work hard at keeping up the numbers.

CHILDREN

It is also expected that there will be a good reduction for children, say aged two to ten, but you may choose other ages. For the under twos it is not usual to charge anything, but you will be expected to heat up the baby food and bottles in the microwave. The parents provide the baby food, though you should keep something for emergencies. Some B&Bs have a separate children's meal – say, at 7 o'clock. If served out of doors, it saves a lot of clearing up. It needs to be supervised and probably one of the parents would be willing. This arrangement needs to be confirmed with the parents, because some French people prefer their children to eat at the adult table even if it is not till 8 o'clock. In this case small children may be put to bed after the main course. The children's menu need only have two courses and a drink, so you don't have to charge much. When they eat at the adult table, you just have to rely on them having only a little.

THE HOSTS

Gîtes de France **insist** that the proprietors eat with the guests to give a family atmosphere. Very few do. There are several reasons why this is an impractical idea:

1. Many women are too conscious of their figure to want such a large meal every day.

2. The cook will use a very limited range of recipes week in week out.

3. With more than six guests it needs two staff to cope.

4. If the dishes aren't cleared up as the meal progresses, you'll be up till all hours.

5. A partial solution is that one of you could join the guests while the other cooks.

   We tried, when possible, to join the table for coffee.

So when do you eat? I'm afraid that in high season you'll be snatching your meals whenever you can. You should be able to have lunch in peace.

Crockery, glassware, cutlery

Things get lost or broken at a fast rate, mostly by yourselves because you're pushed for time. Therefore **do not** use your own good quality stuff. There will often be a stall of white china at markets: it's slight seconds and is amazing value. Hotel quality china is available from cash-and-carries and really is less breakable, plus you'll be able to get replacements easily. Don't have the crockery that is actually made of glass, it's considered cheap. The quantity of everything needs to be **at least** one and a half times the number of people i.e. 12 of everything for 8 people. This allows for breakages or items found to be dirty at the last minute. This does happen. Wine glasses must be considered as totally expendable stock, so buy 19cl goblets and nothing fancy. I'm sure you will have all the table mats, crockery, cutlery and glasses matching, so no one will mind if the serving dishes are odd. Steak knives are commonly used, fish knives and forks appear only if you happen to have them, and doilies are an absolute no-no.

LUNCH

You must be gluttons for punishment. Of course you would only be offering lunch if you are a *table d'hôte*. In fact it's a rare B&B that does lunches, simply because it's seldom asked for unless you are really remote. However, you could offer a packed lunch, which can either be taken away or eaten in a shady spot in your own grounds. Or you could do a salad. If you are offering full board it must be made clear that it is only a light meal, because the midday lunch is still the main meal of the day for some French people.

If you don't offer lunches, what are people to do if staying more than one night? Our guests' usual pattern was to go out in the morning, eat out or have a picnic, return mid-afternoon to spend the rest of the day by the pool, and then eat in. Families with young children, and the occasional couple, do sometimes stay around all day and bought their own picnic. We had a large fridge/freezer for the guests' use. If you provide any form of mini kitchen or barbecue, then it will be used for lunches.

REGIONAL COOKING

French cuisine has a world-wide reputation, so it is with some trepidation that I, an Englishwoman, dare to put down a few words on the subject, the more so as their opinion of my country's cooking is rock bottom as exemplified by the following story. An English B&B proprietor asked her French guests if they wanted dinner that night. 'Oh no,' they said, 'we know the English can't cook'. Naturally I don't accept that opinion. In fact the French need to look to their laurels because high wages are closing restaurants at a rapid rate and the spread of giant hypermarkets is affecting home cooking. Nevertheless the French will expect a good standard at a *table d'hôte*. They think of food in terms of taste rather than nutrition, and will take a keen interest in all that is put in front of them. You will be asked detailed questions like, 'How many eggs in the *crème caramel?*' This will be in contrast to the seeming indifference of the British with their 'very nice', or Americans with their over the top enthusiasm.

Gîtes de France **insist** that the cooking must be 'regional'. This is a concept unknown in the British Isles, whatever the tourist boards say. So you really ought to make the effort to learn some recipes from your region. You may well be at a loss to know what gastronomic region you are in and what the local cuisine is. I'm sure your local French bookshop will have a shelf of cook books, but here is a rough guide to get you started thinking along the right lines.

Regional cooking derives from the climate, and the country can be divided approximately into four areas according to the type of fat used:

- Butter – the largest area, including Paris and the north (with the exception of Alsace-Lorraine), the Atlantic coast, and the east. All areas with a climate suitable for raising cattle. This is the *haute cuisine* so famous all over the world.

- Lard – mostly pigs and geese; the animals of the poor because they can be raised economically. Alsace-Lorraine where the pig dominates; and the centre and south centre down to the Mediterranean where the goose dominates. This is the least well-known cuisine.

- Olive oil – the south east where olives will grow in the poor soil. This is a variation of the Mediterranean cooking we know so well.

- Butter, Lard and Oil – the Pyrénées. A mixture of all three because the Pyrenean mountains stretch from the Atlantic to the Mediteranean and contain many formerly isolated valleys, each of which developed its own specialities.

DINNER (*see Fig. 19*)

Entrée
This is **essential** but keep it simple. Learn a few soups and salads. Soup should be ladled out at the table so as not to spill it. Salads can be either on the plate or a selection in the centre of the table.

Main course
Practise seven recipes over the winter. In the rare event that anyone books demi-pension for a fortnight they won't be taken aback if the same thing appears again. Don't ignore rabbit; it's very popular in France. So are kidneys, but some British don't like offal so don't serve them unless you've confirmed first that it's acceptable. In French cooking the vegetables and the potatoes/rice/pasta are minor accompaniments to the meat or fish. The vegetable element of the meal is provided by salads, and the starch by bread.

Cheese
This is served before the dessert. The French will know the prices of the various types, so go for the middle of the range. Do them the honour of only having French cheeses. No need to have too many. For two people, have

Chambres d'Hôtes Bon Temps
****
****

TABLE D'HOTE
Dîner 25€ (enfants 12€) à 20 heures

Potage/Entrée

Plat du Jour

Fromage

Dessert Maison

¼ l vin & café compris

Uniquement sur réservation
avant 10 heures le matin

Figure 19 The normal number of courses for dinner

two varieties, for three or four people have three varieties, for five and up have a maximum of four varieties; with a good mix of hard, soft, goat's and blue cheeses. Avoid *Emmental*, that's for cooking; and *raclette,* that's for serving hot as a dip at parties. Either put the cheese on a board, English fashion, or go round serving it as in restaurants. Cheese should be removed from the fridge half an hour before use. A lot of the cost is in the wastage, so wrap each piece in foil for storing. Cheese is accompanied by bread or rolls, **not** biscuits, and **no** butter. I notice that you only get cheese **and** a dessert with expensive meals in restaurants now, so it could be omitted. However, some people will ask for cheese instead of the dessert. I can only suggest you keep a pack handy and bring it out if asked; your super dessert is then wasted but at least you have pleased your customer.

Dessert

Learn the French standards which are:

Crème caramel
Mousse au chocolat
Tarte aux pommes

and three more which are not quite so common:

Îles flottantes
Tarte tatin
Clafoutis aux cerises

However I found that not everyone wants a pie in a four-course meal, so I didn't do one very often. Don't worry about buying the pastry; everyone does. Although the rest of the meal should be French-style, you can be more international with the desserts. Tiramasu has had its day, and now the current **in** dessert is *crumble au pomme* (apple crumble). You would find buying the fancy ice creams and frozen gateaux expensive. If you really don't want to have cheese and a dessert, there's a hybrid which consists of serving *confiture de cerises* (cherry jam) with *fromage de brébis* (sheep's milk cheese).

More than once I was asked to provide a birthday cake. So I made a gateau, and added candles if it was for a child. This, of course, was at no extra cost; one has to do the little bit extra.

Coffee

Freshly made real coffee of course, and served in a *demi-tasse* (small cup). For those who say they can't sleep after drinking coffee, you may have to provide tea, herb tea, or decaffeinated coffee. Some British will ask for milk. Since there isn't room for milk in a *demi-tasse*, the solution is to put a small jug of light cream on the table. The 'cash and carries' sell large packs of the little chocolates if you want them.

It is not the French custom to go into another room for coffee, so clear the table as much as possible after the dessert and leave them to it – unless it's an all Brit table and then you can shift them.

Drinks

We tried an aperitif (kir) but found people weren't very interested, so gave it up. You may have a different experience.

'A meal without wine is like a day without sunshine'. So said the French until recently, but general consumption is dropping especially among the young and we have found them to be predominantly modest drinkers at the table. However, wine is still expected to be available with dinner and the cost of this must be included in the price of the meal. Allow ¼-litre per person of an ordinary red table wine. Chill a bottle of white just in case anyone asks for it. Start by buying a *vin ordinaire* in a 5-litre cube at the supermarket until you get acquainted with what is available locally. Then, if you are in a wine-growing area, buy in bulk at a vineyard or local *cave* (wine merchant's). At a vineyard **always** try a sample, and don't buy too cheaply. I regret to say it's the Brits who often drink a lot. Well, it's 'free' if it's included in the price of the meal, isn't it? This poses a dilemma, because what will you do if they ask for some more? One solution is to allow them to bring their own wine to the table, otherwise just give them a little more for the sake of goodwill.

amuse-gueule (m)	cocktail snack	dîner (m)	dinner
apéritif (m)	aperitif	entrée (f)	starter
assiette creuse (f)	soup plate	fourchette (f)	fork
boîte (f)	tin can	fromage (m)	cheese
bougie (f)	candle	louche (f)	ladle
bouilloire (f)	kettle	poêle (f)	frying pan
carafe (f)	decanter	plat (m)	dish
casserole (f)	saucepan	plat du jour	dish of the day
chandelier (m)	candle stick	plat principal	main course
conserve (f)	tinned food	potage (m)	soup
couvert (m)	place setting	régime (m)	diet
cuillère à soup (f)	soup spoon	sel & piovre	salt & pepper pots
demi-tasse (f)	coffee cup	soupière (f)	soup-tureen
dessert (m)	dessert	surgelés (m)	frozen food
digestif (m)	after dinner drink	verre (m)	drinking glass
It would take a book to give all the foods used in cooking.			

Figure 20   Glossary for dinners

Red wine should be served 'at room temperature'. Yes, but what temperature is that? In fact modern central heating and very hot weather are **too warm**. So keep it in a cool room, not the fridge, until required. White wine should be served 'cool'. Yes, but not **too cool**. It will take two hours in a fridge to reach drinking temperature, or three hours if the door is opened frequently. If you're in a hurry, it can be cooled in an ice bucket in 10–20 minutes if the bucket is filled with ice and water up to the neck of the bottle. Tip the bottle upside down for a few minutes if it is not quite covered.

Obviously you must put water on the table but, apart from the cost, there are differing opinions on the merits of tap water and bottled mineral water. Some think tap water is not pure enough; others that water 'straight out of a plastic bottle' is suspect. You'll have your own opinion.

SOME FURTHER POINTS

◆ Give generous portions.

◆ Have meals out of doors if at all possible.

◆ Getting the food to the table hot is absolutely essential. This is not helped by the British etiquette of not starting before everyone is served.

◆ Don't forget to put bread on the table.

Traditionally the French keep the same plate and cutlery throughout the meal. It's polite to finish everything and wipe the plate clean with a piece of bread, unlike Americans where it's polite to leave some. Dishwashing machines mean we are now more lavish with the utensils, but you could tell guests to keep the cutlery from the entrée to the main course, it gives a French feel to the meal and does save on the quantity needed.

DIETS

You will receive many and varied requests. For vegetarians you need to have one dish in the repertoire. It should not be an omelette because only too often that is the only option. If a vegetarian wants demi-pension, don't be a martyr, just say it's not possible. For a diabetic dessert, arrange sliced fruits in a pattern on a large plate; it looks great.

For people with allergies, just do your best. It would help a lot if one had advance warning of special requirements, but that doesn't always happen.

BARBECUE

I do recommend having a barbecue once a week, say Sundays, in high season. We found it very popular. It was the one time when we did eat with our guests, and since the people in our *gîte* invariably came as well, it made for a good crowd. Profitable too, as the food is fairly cheap. Due to the climate, it was only rained off once. We set it slightly earlier at 7pm, and our menu was:

Aperitif (kir or white wine)
Barbecued meats with a buffet
   of salads
One large round of cheese   } second and third helpings encouraged
Big bowl of fruit salad
Coffee
Light red wine (½ litre per person)

You may feel that with a barbecue in the evening, a brunch would be appropriate. This poses all sorts of problems of charging, and timing, and when do you get in the bedrooms, such that I don't see it working.

Have you thought of not doing the barbecue yourselves, and getting some friends to do it? They wouldn't need cooking experience. Then you take the evening off.

GOURMET DINNER

Gourmet Dinner/Candlelit Dinner In The Barn/*Le 14 juillet* – any excuse will do if you want to put on something special, and of course charge more. Proviso no.1 – do you have the skill? Proviso no. 2 – how are you going to charge extra to people who have booked demi-pension? I did warn that demi-pension has its problems. Unless you are an expert chef, it would be very difficult to do an ordinary dinner as well as a special. You need to go to

some good restaurants to find what to serve, but remember that your drinks
have to be included in the price. The wines should be *Appellation d'Origine
Contrôlée/AOC*, i.e. good. A problem with a candlelit dinner is that in the
summer it doesn't get dark till late.

I would be very careful about doing a 'foreign night'. The French are not
keen on other cuisines, and the only ones found occasionally are Vietnamese
and Moroccan.

Have you thought of hiring someone else to cook your gourmet dinner? It
would need an experienced person and they will want paying. Whether hiring
help or not, be careful with the price to make sure you are making a profit.

CHRISTMAS AND NEW YEAR

You may like to do a special meal for these occasions, but the difficulty is in
the advertising to ensure a full house. You'd have to remember to include it
in all your regular advertisements, and in your brochure. It would be very
embarrassing to end up with only two guests. But a full house would be an
immense amount of work, so are you sure?

You are unlikely to attract any French for Christmas, as it's not an
important festival, so you will be doing the full English if at all; which needs
no elaboration here.

Since we have no particular tradition for the New Year, I would go for a
French meal. In this case it **must** start with oysters and champagne and there
should be about six courses. There should be several good wines, and a
digestif to finish/toast the New Year. Apart from the quality of the food and
the conversation, the French judge the success of a meal by the number of
courses and the length of time spent at the table. To make the occasion a
good four-hour affair you could introduce an event between each course, for
instance: a game at the table/poetry reading/music/singalong. I've had such
an occasion recounted to me and told it was a great success.

Again, be careful with the price to make sure you are making a profit. You
would have to decide whether these events are to be a family event or

whether you want to make money. For making money you can't have too many free-loading relatives and friends unless they are really going to work hard.

SUPPLIES

The shopping is no different from that for a normal household except that it's three or four times the quantity. So it's the supermarket once a week (lunchtime is best for speed) and the local shops in between. Markets are good for vegetables but they're only one morning a week. Local butchers have superb quality but at a price. I would have an account at a cash-and-carry for those few things not available in the supermarkets, but otherwise their prices are not competitive and anyway the storage of bulk goods is a real problem in a hot climate. Tea bags are **much** cheaper in the UK.

Defective goods can be returned within seven days for a full refund, but do go back to the original shop because many of what appear to be chain shops are in fact franchises.

FROZEN FOOD

The French are very censorious about frozen food from the aspect of both taste and safety. You are **not allowed to freeze animal products** except with proper fast freezing equipment, which is unlikely in a B&B. In fact, they put great emphasis on produce being fresh, so you should not even serve frozen vegetables unless home grown. There is no restriction on products bought already frozen, which can be a life saver, since you need to have an emergency supply of practically everything for the day when all hell breaks loose.

RESERVATION

Some people think a *table d'hôte* is a restaurant and meals can be ordered when you sit down at the table. We **never** offered dinner unless the reservation was made before 10am. We certainly lost business this way, and the reservation requirement had to be emphasized to clients when they booked. If you feel you can cope with last-minute orders, all well and good. You'd need to rely a lot on the freezer, and if everyone is at the same table, the late arrivals will be having a different menu. This happens all the time in a restaurant of course. Another way is always to cook two extra portions; it would probably pay if your business is largely one-night stays.

THE CHEF

Don't be overawed by the thought of the cooking. It's not like having a dinner party every night. Of course it does help to have started with only two or three bedrooms and learnt to cope with greater numbers as you go along. One great problem for amateurs is that they are not quick enough. But speed will improve; once you have done the dish twelve times it gets a lot easier. Just wait for the day when you get the back-handed compliment: 'Now we know the English can cook!' and you will feel you have done something to dispel our poor reputation.

TEA

As long as guests arrived before 6pm we offered them a cup of tea or coffee (or beer on a hot day), together with home-made shortbread (there's a homely touch), and a fruit juice for the children. It made a good opportunity for a little chat. The French sometimes refused as afternoon tea is not their custom. After 6.00 we were too busy in the kitchen.

Many guests would like a drink in the afternoon yet you have quite enough to do without being 'on duty' all the time. If there is no tea making facility in the bedroom it is a good idea to have a beverage trolley in the lounge, with a kettle and everything in packet form. Keeping it clean and topped up is all more work of course.

Last thing at night some French like a *tisane* (herbal tea). It is believed to promote a good night's sleep, rather like the Ovaltine and Horlicks of a couple of generations back. Leave the necessary facilities on the landing; they should include sugar but not milk. I came across the *tisane* somewhere I stayed and rather liked it. It's these little touches that mean so much.

TIPS FOR MAKING IT PAY

◆ Keep a careful watch on the costs of each portion of food.

◆ Serve meals out of doors if possible; it's such a novelty that people concentrate less on what they're eating.

◆ Let people make their own hot drinks.

TIP FOR IMPROVING YOUR FRENCH

◆ Buy a French recipe book and try out some new dishes. (Note that the French measurements *cuillère à café* and *cuillère à soup* are the English tea spoon and table spoon).

8

Finance and Administration

FINANCE

To buy a property substantial enough for a B&B, most purchasers under 50 will need a mortgage, even though transferring from the high priced UK to lower priced France. Whether this is so or not, there could be extensive restoration necessary, and the funds may have to be borrowed. Make out a detailed financial plan which should allow for very little B&B income in the first two years. It should include furnishing and equipment and some advertising. How does it look? Have you got enough capital or do you need a loan?

The easiest loan to obtain will always be a mortgage on the property. There are no building societies in France; mortgages are from banks. Provided you don't want more than 50 per cent and can cope with a ten-year repayment period, there should be no difficulty. Mortgages for 25 years are hard to get anyway. If asking for more than 50 per cent the bank will enquire into your personal income, otherwise they might not trouble you. There will be fees both to the *notaire* and the bank for setting it up, but there is seldom a penalty for early repayment. The process should be faster than the UK because they are not waiting around for a favourable survey. The monthly payments will be taken direct from your account and they will insist on insurance. You could always ask to increase the mortgage later on for further improvements or a swimming pool. Naturally, if you default, the property will be repossessed and sold at auction, probably for a lower figure than an estate agent would achieve.

Some British banks and building societies will lend on foreign properties, though they will want a survey and may not be too happy about you disappearing from their shores.

Obviously you mustn't have too much debt, but don't struggle on without any. You'll get the business on a profitable footing much faster by borrowing some money for improvements, rather than waiting to save it. The interest is allowable as a business expense.

EARLY DIFFICULTIES

It is most unlikely that your first two years will make a profit, but by the third year you should at least have an operating profit even if you aren't paying off any debt. However, if things still don't look too good or you hit a bad patch don't give up too soon. Rigorously cut back on all expenses except profitable advertising and see if you can't hang on for one more year. I'm sure it will come right.

GRANTS

Grants for renovation are only available to members of the official associations and typically are for 30 per cent of the building work. But the amounts and conditions vary between *départements*, so make enquiries at an early stage. You may be able to get additional money for architects' fees, improvements to the environment, or extra facilities such as a swimming pool. It is not possible to get a grant for a new building or for the furnishing. You have to submit quotations in a particular format with the application, so ask for details before speaking to builders; and the approval will take some time. The documents are sent to the *Conseil Général* (local authority) for scrutiny, and if you are in a hurry to begin the work, you can try applying to them direct for permission to start ahead of the formal approval. It is also possible for the grant to cover the cost of materials for doing the work yourself. The money will not be released until the rooms are furnished ready for use and inspected, so you have to fund it yourself until then. With the letter of approval in hand, your bank will probably look favourably on a loan. These grants are well worth having, but since they are taxed as income, try to get the money in the earlier years when you aren't making much. There are extra grants for farmers and historic buildings.

PRICES

The basic source of income is the room charge, generally quoted for two people. Buy several guide books and make a thorough survey of what others with similar accommodation to your own are charging, and fix yours in the middle. **Do not** down grade yourself – possibly your establishment has some special features. And **do not** start low with the intention of raising the price later; it alienates existing customers. However, don't be afraid to raise it a little each year; it's so easy to let it drift, and people will expect an increase anyway.

Somehow you have got to make your B&B stand out from everyone else's, and there are plenty of ideas in this book; price alone isn't as important as people make it out to be. At four *épis* a high price is part of the perception of a quality product. However, the UK has a reputation for wickedly high prices in hotels and restaurants and French prices are certainly lower – and so they ought to be with most property at half the price. The following example of a tariff (*see Fig. 21 – English; Fig. 22 – French*) shows slightly above-average prices for three *épis*.

You should also ascertain what the hotels in your area are charging. You will find that the ordinary sort of town centre hotel is really a restaurant with a few rooms to let and no other facilities for guests. They make their money from the restaurant, so their charge will be low. Yours should be

Chambres d'Hôtes BonTemps

TARIFF 2008

Room charge per night	Jun, Jul, Aug, Sep	Other months
One person	€50	€40
Two people	€65	€55
Three people	€80	€70

All rooms have a private bathroom
Generous continental breakfast included

Babies aged 0–2 free
Cot and high chair are available

Children aged 3–10 €15 (in room with 2 adults)

Meals: Lunch €12 ... 2 courses with beverage or picnic hamper
Dinner €25 ... 4 courses with ¼ lt table wine and coffee
Children aged 3–10: Lunch €6, Dinner €12

Pension & Demi-pension (minimum 3 nights) – 10%

Reservation: €10 per room per night or €15 for pension and demi-pension
The reservation fee will be refunded if cancellation is received at least 8 weeks before arrival

Also 2 self-catering cottages for 4 people ... please ask for tariffs

Figure 21   Price list in English

Chambres d'Hôtes BonTemps

TARIFF 2008

Chambre par nuit	juin, juillet août, sept	autres mois
1 personne	50€	40€
2 personnes	65€	55€
3 personnes	80€	70€

Toutes nos chambres ont salle de bain privatif
Petit déjeuner copieux compris

Bébés de 0 à 2 ans gratuits
Lit pour bébé et chaise haute disponibles

Enfants de 3 à 10 ans 15€ dans une chambre avec 2 adultes

Repas Déjeuner 12€ ... 2 plats avec boisson ou Panier pique-nique
Dîner 25€ ... 4 plats, ¼ lt vin & café compris
Enfants de 3 à 10 ans: Déjeuner 6€, Dîner 12€

Pension & Demi-pension (minimum 3 nuits) – 10%

Réservation 10€ par nuit par chambre ou 15€ pour pension & demi-pension
L'acompte sera remboursée si l'annulation est faite plus de 8 semaines avant l'arrivée

Aussi 2 gîtes indépendants pour 4 personnes ... demandez nos tarifs

Figure 22   Price list in French

higher than this, even though you are 'only' a B&B, and remember, they will not be including breakfast. A local three-star hotel in its own grounds is a different matter and you will probably like to be a little below this unless you have a very special building.

Always show your prices in euros and resist giving a sterling conversion because the rates do change over the course of a year. Remember, you can always accept sterling cheques by looking up the exchange rate when people pay. (This is available on www.xe.net/currency or www.travelex.co.uk) If you do give away the fact that you have a sterling account, you must **never** cash cheques for people.

With one or two bedrooms you could claim there are practically no extra costs and you are only charging your time, so the cost can be low. This is not realistic because you have put at the guests' disposal the entire establishment of your home which costs a great deal.

Sometimes a family turns up and begs you to take them in, even with mattresses on the floor, anything. You sympathise, but be careful. What will you charge when you have been put to a lot of trouble, but it still ends up with a sub-standard service? Discuss prices **before** you agree.

FILLING THE ROOMS

The first twelve months are tough and not many B&Bs achieve an occupancy greater than 10 per cent for the year. This will come as a blow if the finances are already overstretched and you were confidently expecting 65 per cent, as one couple were. This 10 per cent won't even pay the costs, so you need to budget for a loss in the first year. After that you **must aim for a 30 per cent occupancy** for the year before you can feel the business is established and you are getting a proper return for the investment and your labour. In the country you could find that you only have a summer season and you never exceed this figure. Even in a large village with an all-year clientele it's difficult for a B&B to exceed 50 per cent occupancy.

The year could look like this:

	In the country	In a village centre
January	0%	30%
February	0% (own holiday)	0% (own holiday)
March	10%	40%
April	15%	40%
May	20%	60%
June	50%	60%
July	95%	95%
August	95%	95%
September	50%	60%
October	15%	60%
November	5%	30%
December	5%	30%
Whole year	Average = 30%	Average = 50%

So there is a huge amount of unused capacity and your ingenuity in filling it will make a big difference to the balance sheet. If you close the usual period is from Toussaint (beginning of November) to Easter. Or just be resigned and only keep one bedroom open.

Ideas for out of season:

◆ A big reduction in price.
◆ Three nights for the price of two.
◆ Classes in all sorts of subjects.
◆ Notice on the gate saying '*ouvert*'.
◆ A big pitch for Christmas and New Year.
◆ Free champagne for a birthday.

BOOKING (*see Fig. 23*)

You must have a **foolproof** reservation calendar. If you double book, the customer will, quite rightly, make one hell of a fuss.

A good word to say about the British is that they are the best in the world for booking early. You may get the first firm booking for the following

---

Chambres d'Hôtes BonTemps

****

****

FORMULAIRE DE RESERVATION
BOOKING FORM

Nous vous proposons de nous communiquer votre réservation par téléphone ou par e-mail immédiatement; nous la garderons 15 jours sous réserve de réception de votre acompte.
We suggest you phone or e-mail your reservation immediately and it will be held for 14 days pending arrival of your deposit.

Nom ....
Name

Adresse ....
Addresse

Tél .... E-mail ....

Date d'arrivée .... No. de nuits ....
Date of arrival   *No. of nights*

No. de personnes .... Ages si moins de 18 ans ....
No. of people   *Ages if under 18*

Nombre de chambres demandé: 1 pers ....
No. of rooms required   2 pers ....
                                 3 pers ....

Lit pliant .... Lit pour bébé ....
Folding bed   *Cot*

Pension   OUI/NON   Demi-pension   OUI/NON
              yes/no   *yes/no*

Si vous n'êtes pas en pension ou demi-pension, voulez vous le dîner le premier soir ? OUI/NON
If not pension or demi-pension, would you like dinner on your first night?   *yes/no*

Montant de l'acompte ci-joint ....
Amount of deposit enclosed

Vos autres commentaires ....
Any other comments

                        ....

Signature .... Date ....

Figure 23 Booking form

season as early as October, but the prime month is January. Next come most other nationalities who reckon that around Easter is time enough. Last are the French – after Easter and right into June still looking to book up the family holiday. I'm told it is tempting fate to book too early; after all, the worst might happen. However, there is a worldwide tendency to book later and later.

After a couple of years, and if you keep a check on the numbers, you will know by the end of March how the season is going to compare with last year.

No deposit received = no firm booking. **Be absolutely firm** about this, even with people you know well. If you are asked to hold a provisional reservation, say firmly it's only for two weeks. If you allow people to dither, it can mean losing an alternative good booking.

Gîtes de France recommend asking for a deposit of 25 per cent, but 15 or 20 per cent or a fixed amount are more usual. When people send the wrong amount, don't be pedantic about getting it right: the object is the firm commitment. At least it does mean there is a little money coming in during the first three months of the year. In particular, don't let a large group mess you about: the larger the group, the more possibilities for a problem (*see Fig. 24 for a model booking receipt*).

Chambres d'Hôtes BonTemps

****

****

Date

Received from ....

Address ....

The Sum of £......... ....

Reservation for ....

....

....

Your hosts, John and Jane, have an extensive knowledge of the area and will be pleased to help plan your visits to places of interest.

Signed

Figure 24   A receipt form

We tried to get a credit card facility from our bank, but the charge was much too high for our little business. This needs solving because we could only accept French and British cheques. Even cheques from other euroland countries attract a charge and I understand that cheques may be withdrawn altogether soon. I know there are agencies out there on the internet who arrange money transfers but they are expensive. For bookings from other countries ask for a cheque in their own currency. Then put it aside, and at the end of the stay make out the final bill for the whole amount and tear up the original cheque. If you don't ask for a deposit, people will be inclined to wonder if they really have got a firm reservation. Send receipts promptly, either using a bought pad or produce your own.

Be very careful on dates because the French reckon them differently. You will already know that our fortnight (14 nights) is their *quinzaine* (15 days). Similarly our seven-day-week is their *huitaine* (eight days).
Therefore:
  English booking for four days = four nights
  French booking for four days = three nights

CANCELLATIONS

Cancellations are a great bugbear, not that there's anything to be done about them. You just hope for another booking to emerge. So it might, but it was never as good: either less people or fewer nights. People not showing up and forgetting to let you know are even worse. Of course it will be those who have made a last-minute reservation with no time to send the deposit. It didn't happen often and I'm afraid it was mostly the French. Well, it is their country and they know they can easily find somewhere else. It is counter productive to say that the room will only be held until 6pm; there is practically no chance of getting anyone else at that late hour. It's even more infuriating if they have booked dinner. A proprietor told me the only time in 15 years he ever lost his temper in front of customers was just such an occasion.

PAYING

After the deposit, the remainder can be paid:

1. In full in advance. This would have to be stipulated on the booking form. Only possible with an entirely foreign clientele and if casual arrivals are not accepted. The French **will not** pay in advance; you lose custom if you try.

2. On arrival. In the flurry of a warm greeting it does come across as a bit mercenary. So only ask this of those who have not paid a deposit.

3. During the stay. If you don't accept cards they have to pay in cash. They may ask for a bill in advance in order to withdraw money from a cash point.

4. On leaving. Administratively this is much the simplest because the bill can include all the meals and any extras. We didn't have anyone leave at 4am without paying.

Accepting sterling cheques on the last day is risky in theory because they will probably be over the £100 guarantee limit. You could ask to see their passport if you are worried, but in fact we never did have a cheque bounce.

La note

This is the equivalent of our bill. It should show your establishment's name and address (have a rubber stamp), and the customer's name and address and the date. Then it should itemise their room charges and meals and any extras, deduct any deposit paid, and show the final balance to pay.

La facture

This is the equivalent of our invoice and you are obliged to provide it if asked. We never were, but kept a pad of forms just in case. They have to be made out to a special format, so ask your accountant what has to be included.

TELEPHONE

France Télécom is the national company but it is being challenged by others. This is your umbilical chord to the outside world via you and your computer. It's more businesslike however to have your own answerphone rather than the service provided by the telephone company.

In spite of email, a lot of business is still done on the telephone. Ideally it should be manned from 8am to 10pm, which is simply not possible with so few of you. But you must achieve as much coverage as possible or you will lose bookings, especially last-minute ones. A cordless extension can be carried with you wherever you go on the premises and it can be handed to clients for their incoming calls, of which there will be a fair number. (*For 'telephone' French, see Fig. 25.*)

à bientôt	see you soon	faux numero	wrong number
allô (*not* allô, allô)	hello	horloge parlante	speaking clock
annuaire	directory	il n'est pas la	he's out
c'est à quel nom?	what name is it?	ne quittez pas	hold on
c'est écrit?	how is it spelt?	pages jaunes	yellow pages
c'est noté	that's noted	quel âge à l'enfant?	how old is the child?
coup de téléphone	phone call	qui est à l'appareil?	who is speaking?
coupé	cut off	raccrocher	to hang up
excusez moi de	excuse me for	rappeller	to call back
vous déranger	disturbing you	téléphoner	to call

Figure 25   On the telephone

COMPUTER

I wouldn't think anyone starts in business these days without one. Maybe you're bringing it from the UK, in which case it will be already set up with English programmes and QUERTY keyboard. These items are only available in France in specialist shops, otherwise they sell the French versions. If your French is shaky, you may have difficulty with the instructions, and if you are used to an English keyboard, a different one will drive you to distraction. What's more, you'll have difficulty with a helpline without fluent French.

Although potential customers may have seen your web site and there is a booking form, they will invariably contact you by email with a question or two. I think it's mostly to check that you really exist. In fact the majority of contact with clients before they arrive is now via email. If you have some standard letters ready drafted in French and English it's quick to reply.

Tip of the day: only the 'True Type' fonts support the euro symbol.

SNAIL MAIL

Letter writing is obviously a dying art, we had one preliminary enquiry by letter in ten years. On the other hand you have sometimes got to write back as there are all sorts of matters to be sorted out, and occasionally people can't be reached any other way. (*For 'Post Office' French see Fig. 26.*) For really important letters, such as cancelling a standing order or making a complaint, the *lettre recommandée avec avis de réception/LR/AR* is obligatory and is widely used. Difficult letters should be in French: if it's legal that nice *notaire* will do it for you, or the tourist office, or a neighbour, or a last resort is to pay a translation service. But for writing it yourself here are some useful phrases (*Fig. 27*).

Boîte Postale xxx/BD xxx	PO Box xxx
carnet	book of 1st class stamps
cedex	system for very large users
code postale	post code
expéditeur/exp	from
facteur	postman
faire suivre	please forward
paquet	parcel
par avion	airmail
la poste	post office
lettre recommandé	recorded delivery
lettre recommandée avec avis de réception	recorded delivery with signed return slip
service économique	second class post
service prioritaire	first class post
surtaxe	postage due
timbre vert	2nd class stamp

The post codes consist of the department numbers (they are in alphabetical order), followed by the town number. The chief town is always '000'. Thus '01000' is the chief town in the department of 'Aine', and '01640' is a village in that department.

Figure 26   The Post Office

INSURANCE

All property in France must be insured, whether there is a mortgage or not, but you will need further public liability insurance. Cover should be for the following:

Openings and endings in decreasing order of formality

le 29 février 2008

Monsieur le Maire
Veuillez agréer, Monsieur le Maire, l'expression de mes sentiments respectueux.
Veuillez agréer, Monsieur le Maire, l'assurance de mes sentiments distinguées.
Veuillez recevoir, Monsieur le Maire, mes salutations distinguées.

Monsieur,
Je vous prie, Monsieur, d'accepter l'expression de mes sentiments les meilleurs.
Recevez, Monsieur, mes sentiments les meilleurs.

Chère Madame,
Veuillez croire, chère Madame, à l'assurance de mes sentiments distingués.
Je vous prie de croire, chère Madame, à l'expression de mes meilleurs sentiments.
Veuillez croire, chère Madame, à mes sentiments très cordiaux.
Avec mes sentiments les meilleurs.
En attendant le plaisir de faire votre connaissance.

Chère Madame Dubois,
Cordialement.

Cher Jean,
Amicalement

Figure 27   Writing letters

- The hosts, their family and animals.

- All the buildings and fixed equipment such as swings and sports installations.

- Equipment for the guests' use such as bicycles, table-tennis, badminton.

- *Table d'hôte* and the risk of food poisoning (this is obligatory).

- Activities organized by the proprietors away from the premises such as visits, hiking, riding and transportation to these.

- Swimming pool and its machinery.

- Potentially dangerous features such as a lake, river, mill pond.

A particular problem for B&B owners is that you cannot insure against theft by the guests without a full hotel insurance, the reason being that you have invited them in; they didn't break in. Discuss this with your insurers because it is a worry if you have any antiques. There are the same problems of under insurance as in the UK if the premiums are not increased every year. If you make a claim, do not sign that they have paid up in full until a good time afterwards, in case anything else turns up. Insurers will refuse to pay for a chimney fire if you cannot produce a certificate that it has been swept in the past 12 months.

ACCOUNTANT

The French income tax forms are complicated and are naturally written in the French version of officialese. You'll never manage it correctly by yourself. The alternative to employing an accountant is to go to the tax office during March and they will do it for you at no charge. They also have a half day's *permanence* (attendance) in every commune for that purpose.

This may suffice for the first year or two and if your affairs are straightforward, but it is much better to employ an accountant from the start. Once the business is registered at the chamber of commerce, it is **essential**. Ask all the British residents you know if they can recommend someone. It is not necessary for the accountant to be local as everything can be sent by mail or email. If it's a British national, then they can handle your foreign business as well.

There exists in France a service unknown in the UK called *Centre de Gestion des Entreprises*. It is a government organisation and their function is to help small firms. They also act as accountants and are situated in most small towns. They are very helpful but are unlikely to speak English and are not conversant with international taxation.

I'm afraid my bookkeeping only ran to a simple double entry book, totalled monthly. Then I had to submit all the bills stapled together, month by month, and copies of the bank account were obtained direct. This is not very sophisticated and your accountant may demand more or recommend a suitable computer programme. One good thing is the books are done in February, well out of season.

For a substantial business run from your own home you will be able to claim 80 per cent of electricity, water, gas, telephone and *Taxe Foncière* as business expenses, plus 50 per cent for the car. I would argue that the 80 per

annulation (f)	cancellation	quinzaine (f)	fortnight
annuler	to cancel	reçu (m)	receipt
arrhes (f)	deposit	répondeur (m)	answerphone
assurance (f)	insurance	réservation (f)	reservation
bénéfice (m)	profit	saison (f)	season
calendrier (m)	calendar	bas saison	low season
congé (m)	leave	haute saison	high season
complet	full	hors saison	out of season
comptable (m)	accountant	sans fil (m)	cordless (phone)
disponible	available	séjour (m)	stay
hébergement (m)	lodging	semaine (f)	week
huitaine (f)	week	subvention (f)	grant
jour (m)	day	tarif (m)	tariff
jour férié	public holiday	télécopie, fax (m)	fax
ordinateur (m)	computer	téléphone (m)	phone
pension	full board	vacance (f)	holiday
demi-pension	half board	vacances scolaires	school holiday
perte (f)	loss	week-end (m)	week-end
portable (m)	mobile phone		

Figure 28 Glossary

cent for the telephone should be increased now. The utility bills are paid by direct debit, but this can lead to the complacency of not scrutinising them closely before they are paid and you could miss a nasty surprise somewhere. (*For a general administration glossary, see Fig. 28.*)

TIPS TO MAKE IT PAY

◆ Only borrow the amount you are sure you can afford.

◆ Investigate grants.

◆ Accept sterling cheques.

◆ Except for last minute bookings, do not accept reservations without a deposit.

◆ Make a target of 30 per cent occupancy for the year.

TIP TO IMPROVE YOUR FRENCH

◆ Buy a dictating machine for less than £20 and listen to yourself reading French.

9

Keep it Clean

CLEANING

I hope you like housework because there will be a lot of it. I once saw a B&B advertised as being 'clean'. Cheeky. Was it to imply that most B&Bs are not? Of course you have got to be and, I admit, cleaner than most of us are in our own homes, since there is no leeway for anything otherwise in a commercial premises. 'There's a hair in the shower and it's not mine' says Mrs Guest. Not in our establishment, thankfully, though lapses do occur and you will be covered with shame. There's nothing for it but to apologise and attend to the problem straight away. Bedrooms and bathrooms need a quick clean every day (ten minutes) and a thorough clean for new guests. Hotels allow 20 minutes for changeovers; I doubt if we achieved that. The family room for four took an hour if there was a cot or folding bed to be put up or dismantled.

Sometimes guests made their own beds, which was nice, but if asked I always insisted we would do it. Make the beds very neatly with hospital

117

corners. The public rooms need cleaning every day. You have to **insist** that people vacate their room by 10am or you'll never get done by lunch time. If the cleaning runs into the afternoon, the guests could arrive, and the rooms may not be ready. It happened once. I sat them down with a cup of tea, and had to think fast for a good excuse. Some B&Bs stipulate that guests must not arrive before 4pm. We found that 2pm was alright because few actually came at that time; most arrived between 4 and 6pm.

MAINTENANCE

Everything broken or damaged must be seen to **immediately**. A German guest complained bitterly about the French on this matter and said it was the reason he'd chosen a proprietor with an English sounding name from the holiday guide. So keep the reputation up to teutonic standards! Admittedly, keeping all those bathrooms functioning gave us more grief than all the other rooms put together; we seemed to need a resident plumber. With careless use something was always going wrong. It helps to keep spares of as many items as possible. I'm afraid the strong sunlight of southern France does a lot of damage to fabrics and furnishings and that's one reason why shutters are kept closed much of the time.

Even if there aren't many guests in the winter, or even if you close, there's little respite. Make a list of 'Things To Do This Winter'. It should include all the regular maintenance, the shopping to upgrade the rooms, the 'spring' cleaning, and the redecorating. It will be quite a list, and you won't get through it, but do try. My own nomination for the one thing that gives the impression of sparkling cleanliness is . . . clean windows.

LINEN

You probably never gave it much thought before. From now on it will loom large in your consciousness. If the good news is that French bed sizes are the same as UK, the bad news is that their linen is quite different. You will probably bring what you already have, but it will not be enough and sooner or later it needs replacing. The big supermarkets have 'white sales' in January and February which are good for curtains, bedspreads, pillows, duvets – all things where matching replacements won't be wanted. The mail order catalogues also have good special offers at that time.

Linen

Wash under-blankets & machine washable bedspreads

Dry-clean bedspreads, duvets, curtains, & blankets on a two- or three-year rotation

Turn out linen and cleaning cupboard and clean

Most pillows with man-made fillings can be washed, or at least wash the covers

Check all linen for mending

Bathrooms & WCs

De-scale chrome fittings and shower heads

Clean wall tiling & shower cubicles

Scrub tiled floors

Freshen up tiled joints with joint whitener

Wash shower curtains

Check any gas heaters well before the first guest arrives

Check for dripping taps and leaking ball valves

Bedrooms & Corridors

Brush ceilings and plastered walls with cobweb brush

Vacuum textured walls such as stone, brick or crepi

Move all furniture and clean behind

Vacuum inside wardrobes and drawers

Turn mattress at the very least once a year and vacuum both sides

Treat stains on rugs & carpets

Clean mirrors & difficult-to-reach windows

Clean light fittings

Check coat hangers & room keys

Public Rooms

Clean walls, ceilings, windows, lights, and move furniture as for bedrooms

Wash removable upholstery covers or clean with proprietary product

Turn out store cupboards & clean

Throw away old tourist literature

Dry-clean curtains every year if there is an open fire

Have fire extinguisher verified & check that smoke detectors function

Check games for missing pieces; tidy library

Remove indoor plants to somewhere warmer if room is not heated

Have chimney swept

Kitchen

Brush walls & ceiling with cobweb brush

Wash light shades & fluorescent covers

Scrub wall tiling

Turn out larder & throw away old stock

Check home made preserves left over from last year

Defrost freezer & put on one side products nearing expiry date and leftovers for using up
yourselves

Clean cooker, fridge, dishwasher, washing machine

Wash all furniture & fittings

Renew cooker hood filter

Scrub floor

Have boiler serviced & fire extinguisher verified

Update recipe file

De-scale appliances & check cups & teapots for staining

Figure 29   Aide memoire for winter maintenance and cleaning

Sheets

The French have stayed with cotton more than the UK. There's no doubt that it is best and good hotels all over the world have cotton. It should be good quality or it will feel like being in hospital. Quality is defined by the number of threads to the inch: standard is 180, the best is 300. However, a B&B is not the Ritz and poly-cotton is so much easier to wash, to dry, and to iron. If you have coloured or patterned sheets, the colours will fade with all that washing so you'll never be able to mix in any more, even if available. That's why most people stay with white. The quantity needed varies with the length of stay and how often they are changed, certainly twice a week for grade four. At boarding school we had clean sheets once a fortnight, but times are different now. Start with three sets per bed and see how you get on. I know many people don't iron sheets, and Americans certainly never do, but the French do expect this to be done.

Pillows

A decision to be made before leaving the UK is whether to stay with our rectangular pillows, or to have the French 60×60cm size. Neither the rectangular pillows nor the pillow cases are available in France. It's normal to give two pillows each, but note that the square ones are usually paired with a bolster. Most of the rest of the world doesn't like bolsters. A few guests will bring their own, which reveals their low opinion of what they expect to be provided. In any case have some spares as older people will often ask for a third one, and a feather pillow is sometimes requested.

Under blankets

These are always necessary and they **must** be waterproof on single and folding beds where you expect children. You can have waterproof on adults beds too; after all, small children often get in with their parents, though some people may object. They should be washed frequently so you need some spares.

Duvets and blankets

Again a difference: the British have nearly all changed to duvets. The French not so much. When duvets are used they are accompanied by an ordinary set of sheets along with the duvet and its cover. For a B&B this is a very good idea because washing a duvet cover and a bottom sheet with integral valance is a chore after only one night. But duvets are really too hot in France in the summer so you need some blankets as well, and therefore could consider having blankets only.

Bedspreads

Blankets need a bedspread. Be bold and have something brightly patterned because they are such a dominant feature of the room. You will need a lightweight one for the summer, and a warmer one for the winter. If the winter one is quilted for warmth, this reduces the weight of blankets.

Towels

Yes, lots. It's normal to give a large and a small one per person. The Dutch like clean towels every day. The recommendation is twice a week for grade three, and every day, if used, for grade four. The problem when not changing towels that day is how to get them dry in the greater part of the year when the bathroom isn't heated. The guests will drape them all over the place, even out of the window. Tut, tut, we don't want to look like a shanty town. If they were very wet, I would put them on the line. There should be a matching washable bath mat. Towels are a problem with a swimming pool. Most guests bring their own swimming towels, but you could find your best ones taken outside. Offering swimming towels, gratis, helps.

Table cloths, napkins and serviettes

Cloths rarely last for more than one meal, or you could have mats for dinner. Paper serviettes are alright for breakfast, but for dinner you should have fabric. It's all yet more washing.

CURTAINS

Until recently French homes seldom had curtains; the shutters served the same function. You do need them now for an international clientele.

However, the inward-opening windows make for problems. If the curtains are close to the window you can't have the window open and the curtains closed at the same time. So do try and set the curtains back from the window. Then explain to foreign clients that the shutters really work and in hot weather they should open the windows and latch the shutters only partly shut. Curtains have become more elaborate than they used to be, and expensive. If you have tie-backs it will be you who is tying them back prettily every day; it's all extra minutes when doing the rooms. If the window is overlooked, you'll need net curtains as well, mounted on the frame itself because of the inward opening.

I would be wary of blinds because I'm sure they would get damaged.

LAUNDRY

There was a **lot** of washing and it needed doing **every day** in the season. The machine needs to have minimum wash programmes because a lot of the washing is after only one night. You can just about manage without a dryer in the south, but it is the best way of keeping the towels fluffy. Dryer, or not, you need plenty of washing-line because the guests often wash their smalls or hang up their swimming things. An ironing machine is not a luxury in this situation – not a commercial one, just a domestic flat bed type will make all the difference. You will miss the UK airing cupboard, but really the climate is so much drier that it's not necessary.

If all the laundry is getting on top of you, how about sending it out? If one person is trying to run a B&B on their own, it is the one big time saver that could make the difference between success and utter exhaustion. A laundry will also hire out linen. To find one look in your local shops to see who is an agent for a dry cleaners; that firm will also probably do laundry.

EQUIPMENT AND MATERIALS

Keeping all the machines in working order made for plenty of repair bills. Put the guarantees in a safe place, you'll need them. (*For a list of equipment see Fig. 30.*)

You must watch the cost of cleaning materials because you will use a lot, yet you are highly unlikely to have the storage space for buying in bulk. Those wet wipes are expensive and did you know that white vinegar (at 37 cents a litre) is excellent for cleaning glass shower enclosures? Just wipe it on, then

For Starting Up
Refrigerator
Dishwasher
Washing machine
Domestic cooker
Large chest freezer
Large kettle and coffee machine
Vacuum cleaner
Large microwave
Kitchen robot

Computer
Telephone and answer phone
Electric drill
Sewing machine
Iron and ironing board
Trailer or small van
Ride-on mower ⎫
Strimmer ⎬ if large garden
⎭

Later
2nd vacuum cleaner (1 upstairs, 1 downstairs)
Large larder-type fridge (keep original one for visitors)
Ironing machine
2nd iron and ironing board (for visitors)
Car battery charger (for self and visitors)
Replace cooker with large commercial type with hood
2nd kettle, 2nd coffee machine
Drying machine
2nd washing machine (for self and visitors)
Electric oil filled radiator ⎫
Electric fan heater ⎬ for standby use
Bottle gas heater ⎭
Safe
2 men's, 2 women's bicycles (children's optional)
Gas barbecue
Electric log-cutting machine (if log fire)
Electric garden shredder ⎫
Chain saw ⎬ if large garden
Electric hedge cutter ⎭

Figure 30 The equipment you will need

polish with a clean cloth. The spray for the same job is €3 for 700ml. But only use cheaper substitutes if they don't take extra time. (*For glossary of housekeeping terms see Fig. 31.*)

THE KITCHEN

You have got to be **very careful** in the kitchen:

1. Wash your hands.
2. Don't allow pets in the kitchen.
3. Separate chopping board for meat.

4. Check temperatures of fridge and freezer.
5. And have everything super clean.

Cooking in quantity makes for a lot of fat going down the sink and it'll surely block one day. One of my favourite French words is *catastrophe*, which describes this situation. There is a nifty gadget called a *furet* (ferret) which is basically a screw on the end of a long flexible rod, with a handle to turn it: obtainable from ironmongers it works a treat. Another way is to put *soude caustique* (caustic soda) down the sink. It's toxic stuff but is obtainable from supermarkets. A septic tank needs re-activating afterwards.

SMOKING

You need a policy. The only one I can recommend is to have an entirely non-smoking establishment. I am sure this is acceptable these days so mention it in your publicity. Just one notice on each floor is sufficient to remind people, and then there needs to be something outside the entrance door for the butts so they're not to be scattered all around. A few guests will still smoke in their bedrooms of course. This really can't be helped.

THE WILDLIFE

Most of us Brits are townies and are quite unprepared for this aspect of living in the country. By wildlife, I mean the ones with none, two, four, six, or eight legs: flying, scampering, crawling or slithering indoors. There are so many more of them than we are used to, and keeping them at bay was a constant battle. The trouble is the guests don't understand this. One of the bedrooms was invaded by flying ants. 'No problem,' we say 'we'll spray it while you're having dinner.' 'Oh no,' they say, 'we don't approve of chemicals; we keep a health food shop.' Of course.

In the country rodents are a particular problem. There are many more of them even than in British rural areas. However many cats there are, they won't make an impression on the numbers. At the first evidence of a mouse, clear the drawer or shelf and set a trap. When one is caught, keep setting the trap for a couple of days to see if there is a family. I prefer this to poison because we did have cats. There were a few rats outside, but also another rodent peculiar to the south called a *loir*. In size it's between a mouse and a rat but it has a hairy tail. They eat fruit and seeds, so they don't come into the body of the house, but they love roof spaces and guests can complain about the noise. Get the kind of trap from the ironmonger's that catches them alive and then release the creatures in a wood. For a swarm of bees, try and find a bee keeper because they are a protected species. If a nest can't be reached and for wasps and hornets call the fire brigade. There will be a charge. For other insects you need to have ready an arsenal of repellents. Use a spray at the first sight of a column of marching ants. The guests may complain about mosquitoes; we kept a supply of appropriate products.

abat-jour (m)	lamp shade	nappe (f)	table cloth
alèse (f)	under blanket	nettoyer	to clean
araignée (f)	spider	oreiller (m)	pillow
toile d'araignée (f)	spider's web	taie d'oreiller (f)	pillow case
aspirateur (m)	vacuum cleaner	panier (m)	linen basket
bac à graisse (m)	grease trap	(en) panne	broken
balai (m)	broom	pièce détachée (f)	spare part
balayer	to sweep	pince à linge (f)	clothes peg
cendrier (m)	ash tray	pipi (m)	wee-wee
cintre (m)	coat hanger	poignée (f)	handle
clé (f)	key	porte savon (f)	soap dish
corde à linge (f)	clothes line	poussière (f)	dust
couette (f)	duvet, quilt	propre	clean
housse de couette (f)	duvet cover	ramoner	to sweep a chimney
couverture (f)	blanket	repasser	to iron
crochet (m)	hook	fer à repasser (m)	iron
débarrasser	to clear away	plancheà repasser (f)	ironing board
déshumidficateur (m)	dehumidifier	rideau (m)	curtain
drap (m)	sheet	sale	dirty
drap housse	fitted sheet	savon (m)	soap
drap plat	flat sheet	savonette (f)	small soap
eau de javel (f)	bleach	serpillière (f)	floor cloth
fourmi (f)	ant	serrure (f)	lock
gant (m)	face flannel	serviette (f)	towel, serviette
jeté de lit (m)	bedspread	shampooing (m)	shampoo
lampe (f)	(electric) bulb	tapis de bain (m)	bath mat
lessive (f)	washing powder	torchon (m)	dishcloth
linge de lit (m)	bed linen	traversin (m)	bolster
(en) marche	working	taie de traversin	bolster case
moustique (m)	mosquito	tringle (f)	curtain rod

Figure 31 Glossary

THE WELCOME

First impressions are important, especially the room temperature. In very hot weather it looks thoughtful to have the shutters partially closed to keep the sun out. In cold weather of course the bedroom and bathroom should be warm. Everyone loves freebies. Usually it's a small soap, sachet of shampoo/shower gel, and a box of tissues; all obtainable from the 'cash and carry'. Hotel suppliers have a better quality range but the minimum order is about 500 and there is a hefty delivery charge for 'small' orders. It is best to have individual sachets of these items: people don't like using soaps and bottles that have previously been used by someone else. At grade four, expectations are high and you should provide good quality products, renewed frequently, together with fresh flowers and a bowl of fresh fruit. In most *départements* there should be a free guide to what's on, published either by a local newspaper or the tourist office, and it's a good idea to put one in each room.

TIPS FOR MAKING IT PAY

- ◆ Have only white linen.
- ◆ Buy mostly in the January sales.
- ◆ Have table mats or non-iron tablecloths.

TIP FOR IMPROVING YOUR FRENCH

- ◆ Buy a disc of French songs. You should be able to find Edith Piaf or Jaques Brel.

10

Dealing with Officialdom

On setting up a business in France you will come across their immense bureaucracy. With the added disadvantage of another language, you may find it daunting. However, you must try and understand it because the costs are high and ignorance can lead to paying more than necessary. Although rates and income tax are lower, the high social security payments bring the total to more than the UK. Unfortunately, most taxes and final metered charges for utilities have to be paid in the six months from October to March, which is just when a B&B is receiving least income. There are severe penalties for late payment. Most of you will have been in salaried employment in the UK where all taxes, excepting rates, are paid by the employer. As a self-employed person in France, you will be taken aback by the number of tax demands that keep arriving in the letter-box. The information in this chapter must be considered as only a precis of the situation.

One could wish that the multitude of rules and regulations to which we are subjected should be available in writing in plain French. They are not, and if you ask for information at the tax or social security office, you are likely to get an evasive answer and it will differ between departments. The reason is that jurisprudence, i.e. previous court decisions on the matter, are only binding on the case in hand and not universally. So any official is still free to make their own interpretations.

It doesn't help that neither *chambres d'hôtes* nor *table d'hôte* have a legal definition, therefore officials do vary as to which business category you belong to. Sometimes they will allow you to be a *gîte*, in which case you are just letting part of your own home. But particularly if you have a *table d'hôte*, they will say you are a fully-fledged business, which is quite a different matter. It really depends on the scale of the enterprise. You must go to the *mairie* (town hall) to notify them of your presence before you open.

You will find the French language is choc-a-block of acronyms: *CPAM*, *URSSAF*, *SAMU*, *SMIC*, to name only a few. I know they exist in English too, but I don't think there are quite so many.

CHAMBER OF COMMERCE *(Chambre de Commerce)*

This is not a club as in the UK, instead it is a government office. In France you cannot just open up a business, it **has** to be registered with the *chambre* designated for that trade. For a B&B it is the *Chambre de Commerce* located in your *chef-lieu* (county town).

The point at which you are deemed to be a business and therefore have to register is a very grey area. It depends on whether the B&B is your main income; just two bedrooms is unlikely to provide a living; three is questionable; four or more begins to look more like a business. Registration should be within a fortnight of starting.

However, you will want to delay registering for as long as possible because it triggers all the **obligatory** tax, social security, health and pension payments.

Unless, that is, you need to be working in order to join the health system. The registration only applies to the one type of business named and any ancillary activities. For a B&B you can, for example, charge guests for the hire of bicycles and for laundry. You will also be given a *Siret* number. If you close in the winter you can register for six months only, then unregister and start again next year. The cost of the registration fee may be less than the social security charges, so ask your accountant.

Farmers, even if they are only growing mushrooms, are a protected species with different rules. They belong to the *Chambre d'Agriculture* and can add a holiday letting business to their other activity.

SELF-EMPLOYED *(Entreprise Individuelle)*

For a B&B alone you will probably register at the *Chambre de Commerce* as a self-employed person, and only one of you needs to register. This is the simplest and least expensive, and they will advise you on any formalities. With this format the business and yourself are one legal entity, so you'd better keep up the insurance and not get into debt.

LIMITED COMPANY *(Société à Responsabilité Limité/SARL)*

If the business includes activities additional to the B&B, such as gîtes or other leisure pursuits, you may want to register as a company. It should be done at the time of buying the property and you will need expert advice on this.

PROVING IDENTITY

All French nationals have an **identity card**. Until recently foreigners had a *carte de séjour* but this has been withdrawn on the basis that your own country's card is acceptable. However, the UK is one of the few countries in the EC without them and there are occasions (such as when opening a bank account) when this would be required. A driving licence is usually acceptable and failing that a passport. The latter is not very convenient and they don't contain addresses. A recent utility bill will sometimes be asked for but this could be impossible for a new arrival. All this can be difficult.

Another hurdle is the matter of birth, marriage, etc. certificates. In France everyone has a *livret de famille* (family book) containing all their details. You may be asked for this, so bring all your British certificates and get copies of your children's as well, as it's possible they might have to be officially translated into French.

BANK ACCOUNT *(Compte en Banque)*

Sterling account

I am sure you will want to keep a sterling account because a lot of British guests will like to pay you by cheque. Shop around for a bank with the least transfer charges to France, because there are large differences. Whether transferred to France or not, this income should be declared for income tax purposes and can be treated as a cash payment.

French account

You will have a non-interest-bearing cheque account with a monthly statement as in the UK. It is a criminal offence to allow a cheque to bounce, known as a *cheque en bois*, literally 'a wooden cheque'. In view of this, bank cheque cards are not necessary. However, you will often be asked for identification. Paying by direct debit card (*le plastique*) in now widespread, and there are plenty of cash withdrawal machines. Note that cheques cannot be stopped without a limited number of official reasons, and changing your mind is not one of them. Cheques do seem to be on the way out however and even within the euro zone banks will make an extra charge for those from another country. Credit cards are rare. Although interest rates are now minimal, it's still worth having another savings account.

RATES 1 *(Taxe Foncière)*

This is based on the letting value of the land, whether built on or not. It must be paid by the owner of the land. If you buy mid-year it will be apportioned between the two owners by the *notaire*. Both of these rates 1 and 2 add up to much less than rates in the UK.

RATES 2 (*Taxe d'Habitation*)

This is levied on the resident occupier of the property on January 1st each year. This is tough on the person who moves out on 2nd January but nice for the one who moves in. If the property is not furnished on 1st January, no one has to pay. There are some exemptions or reductions for retired or handicapped people. It is calculated on the size of the buildings and the land.

RATES 3 (*Taxe Professionelle*)

This is the equivalent of our business rate. It is in addition to the other rates and is based on the fixed assets of the business, which in the case of a B&B will be the house. You may succeed in arguing that it's your home and not a business premises.

INCOME TAX (*Impôt sur le Revenu*)

For most income arising in the UK, you can elect for it to be taxed either in the UK or France, and there is a double taxation agreement between the two countries so that tax is not paid twice.

Income tax **must** be paid in France if you **or** your spouse and children stay in the country for more than 183 days (ignoring days of arrival and departure). If you are switching between countries for the first year or two and the B&B is not operating yet, it might be worth arranging your visits such that you don't involve the French taxman. You must register your presence in France at the local *Centre des Impôts*, then you will automatically be sent a tax return form in February. You will find that French income from sources such as salaries, bank interest, pensions, etc. will have already been filled in.

Personal and children's allowances are fairly similar to the UK but you can include elderly relatives as dependants. The fiscal year runs from January 1st, and tax is due on the previous year's income not the current year as in the UK.

VAT *(Taxe sur la Valeur Ajoutée/TVA)*

A registered business is necessarily subject to *TVA* but is exonerated from paying anything when the receipts are below €76,300 for a B&B alone or €27,000 for a B&B with *table d'hôte*. This seems vastly unfair but a *table d'hôte* is a service, not the sale of goods.

If you are assessed for *TVA* you will **have** to have an accountant who will brief you on the details. But before that time keep **all** invoices for capital items: namely, building work and materials and household appliances because they can be fed in to the system for a refund of at least some of the *TVA* paid. After that you have got to get a fully detailed *facture* (invoice) for every half kilo of carrots and packet of loo rolls. This can prove very onerous, especially for a *table d'hôte* which involves shopping most days, but you will have to ask at the checkout before they ring through your items.

The government gets 40 per cent of its revenue from *TVA*. It's cheap to collect too because you will be doing most of the work. The rates that mostly affect a B&B are:

- 5.5 per cent on all food, hotel rooms, restaurant meals, water, domestic renovations

- 28 per cent on cars

- 19.6 per cent on most other goods and services.

You will be issued with a *Siren* number, which with 'fr' added can be used for buying goods direct from the manufacturer in the UK without VAT, but it's hardly worth the palaver.

HEALTH CARE

Internationally the UK is reckoned to be a soft touch for free health care – just turn up and you will be treated. The World Health Organisation may have voted for France in possessing the best health service **but** that doesn't mean you don't need the right documents and to have paid any dues required.

Leaving the British system

Form EHIC (European Health Insurance Card) covers visitors staying up to six months for 'any necessary health treatment'. This has replaced the former E111 and gives a broader cover. It can be obtained from local social security offices.

Form E106 is for those moving to France who are neither working or retired. It lasts for two years, and always starts from 1 January so that could decide your moving date. It gives you the time to sort out a permanent arrangement. However, you must have been working in the UK during the previous two years which could be a problem if the move has been prolonged.

Form E109 is for where one spouse lives and works in UK and the other lives in France.

Form E121 is for those moving to France who are retired or registered disabled. It has no time limitation imposed.

All of the above entitles you to the same benefits as French people and also covers spouses and children. Forms are obtainable from the Social Security headquarters in Newcastle (see the appendix for addresses), and then they must be registered with *CPAM* (see below).

Joining the French system

◆ *Mutuelle* (health insurance company) – residents who are working, even if over retiring age, **must** join a company. A list will be supplied by the *Chambre de Commerce* when the business is registered. Premiums are graded according to income and level of cover chosen (note that most French opt for 100 per cent of cover). This continues after retirement.

◆ Private Insurance – for those to whom none of the above apply. This is obviously expensive and may be refused to those people with pre-existing conditions, but there's no other option at present

◆ *CPAM* (*Caisse Primaire d'Assurance Maladie*) – this is the state social security system with an office in each *département* and they will insist that foreigners must have insurance somewhere. Go along and discuss any problems as they are very helpful (but unlikely to speak English). There is an English helpline on 0820 904 212.

Under all French schemes hospital treatment is free although there is a lodging fee. Also those with a *maladie longue durée* (chronic condition) don't have to pay anything, but pensioners get no concessions. Apart from these specific cases all medical acts have to be paid for at the time: you present your *carte vitale* (a green plastic card) and refunds are sent automatically to your bank. As with the UK you must register with a general practitioner who will give you an *ordonnance* (prescription) for tests, home nursing or specialist treatment as required. For all other paramedics you make your own arrangements and should enquire about refunds.

Customers to your B&B will hopefully have their EHIC and you can direct them to any doctor's office; warn them first that they must pay. They will receive a form for claiming a refund which must be sent to the *CPAM*. Refund cheques will be sent to their home address, in euros of course, or they can go there in person and collect the cash. French pharmacists are trained to attend to minor ailments, so a visit to the chemist might be much simpler.

PENSION *(Assurance Vieillesse)* AND ALLOWANCES

British

State pensions can be paid direct into your French bank account at a favourable rate of exchange. If you aren't yet a 'senior' what plans have you for paying into a scheme somewhere? If you do nothing you could regret it later, and you're unlikely to get anything at all from selling a B&B business as a going concern. To pay voluntary contributions to the state scheme contact the Inland Revenue National Contributions Office (address in Appendix).

If you are relying on any allowances – such as children's, disability, maternity, pensioners' winter fuel – do check whether these will be available in France or you could get an unpleasant surprise.

French

Even if you are over 60/65, and if the business is registered, you **have** to pay into the French system in addition to whatever you have paid in the UK. Since the contributions are not taxed this represents good value for money. If one of the marriage partners does not have any other pension it should be possible to join the same scheme as a *conjoint collaborateur*: do ask for details. There is no choice here, as the *Chambre de Commerce* will inform the appropriate organisation of your arrival.

You will not be eligible for any statutory allowances until you have been working in France, and not on the *Le Black*.

SOCIAL SECURITY

Contributions Sociales
This payment applies to **everyone**, but is dependent on income.

Union de Recouvrement de Sécurité Social et des Allocations Famiales/URSSAF
This is the main social security payment for employed or self-employed people and is in **addition** to health and pension payments; it is also dependent on income.

DRINKS LICENCE *(Licence Débit de Boissons)*

All *chambres d'hôtes* **must** have a licence, even if only serving breakfasts. The licences are in four categories and cover the sale of beverages and alcoholic drinks. For breakfasts only you need a Category 1 Licence (*Licence de Boissons Sans Alcool*), which allows the sale of all non-alcoholic beverages.

A *table d'hôte* needs a Category 2 Licence (*Petite Licence Restaurant*). This allows you to serve all beverages in Category 1 plus Category 2 which includes non-distilled drinks such as wine, beer, champagne and cider.

Ask at the town hall where to obtain these licences; it will probably be a *tabac*. It's a simple matter of giving your name and address; there is no fee and they last permanently. Both of these licences **only** allow beverages and drinks to be consumed on the premises and they **must not** be charged extra. In addition the alcoholic drinks **must** accompany a meal.

If you want to keep a wine cellar and charge for the drinks, then you will need a Category 3 or 4 licence. These are expensive, involve much negotiation with officialdom and also have tax implications.

MOTOR VEHICLES

EU driving licences are valid in France, but if you have an accident, there can be problems, so it is better to change to a French *permis de conduire* (driving licence). This is only possible after you have a *Carte de Séjour*. Other nationalities have to take lessons and a test. On buying a car you will be issued with a *Carte Grise* (log book) which, together with the insurance and driving licence, should be carried at all times in the car. There is a severe points system for offences, and in the extreme you could lose your licence. This would be a serious drawback for the business, but there is a jokey little car called a *véhicule sans permis* that can be driven without a licence. All vehicles over four years old must have a *Contrôle Tecnique* (MOT) every two years. Insurance and no claims bonuses are similar to the UK but more expensive because of their high accident rate and the amount of car theft.

The vehicle tax has been abolished, and from 2009 the present vehicle numbering system which identified the *département* will disappear. This is a pity, because when you got to know the numbers it was a useful talking point with newly arrived guests.

TV LICENCE *(Service de la Redevance de l'Audiovisuel)*

When a TV is bought in France, the shop will notify the licensing authority and a demand is sent automatically. It must be paid even if you only receive British programmes via satellite or even if the set is not in use. It accompanies the *Taxe d'Habitation* and has the same exemptions.

THE POLICE *(Les Gendarmes)*

We found them courteous and helpful and they found our car within three days of it being stolen. Then the insurance company paid for a first class train ticket to go and collect it. Then when we went to the wrong police station a police driver took us to the correct one. And one thing more: the parents of one of the *gendarmes* came and stayed for a week in our *chambres d'hôtes*. Go along and make yourself known.

To help security and fight terrorism, foreign paying guests must fill in a *Fiche Individuelle de Police* (individual police slip) with their details. *Gîtes de France* or the *gendarmerie* will provide a sample for copying. These should be kept for six months.

FIRE AND AMBULANCE *(Sapeurs Pompiers)*

Fortunately I haven't had first-hand knowledge of these services but I'm told they are good. Unlike the UK, the emergency ambulances in the country are red and are run by the fire service. In a small town it is voluntary and the members will include one of the local doctors. The non-emergency ambulances are run quite separately by private companies.

You can also call the *pompiers* when the house is flooded, if the roof is damaged by a storm or falling trees, to rescue trapped animals and for chimney fires. So give the *pompiers* a good tip when they call in to sell their calendar at Christmas!

ELECTRICITY, GAS AND WATER

These are at present all fully or partially government owned but are in the process of becoming open to outside enterprises. There will be a mid-year bill estimated on last year's consumption and an end of year bill from the meter reading. There are several electricity tariffs, with a worthwhile reduction if you limit your winter consumption. But discuss this in the light of your requirements, especially if you stay open in the winter and use electricity for heating or hot water. The water bill is reduced if you don't have mains drainage. They like payment by direct debit and it's safer, because there is a big charge if you 'inadvertently' get cut off.

THE BLACK *(Le Noir, Le Black)*

It is rife in France, but **don't have anything to do with it.** It's not your country, and it's not your problem. You wouldn't be able to declare any payments as business expenses.

Furthermore the penalties are:

◆ €30,000 fine and two years in prison.

◆ If a person working for you has an accident at work you would be liable for all medical and hospital bills.

◆ The income tax inspectors will asses the persons concerned for back taxes.

WHERE TO GET HELP IN FRANCE

You don't need to think the French themselves get it right all the time either. So you'll not be alone. Don't worry or spend any sleepless nights. Just do it, or pay it, and see what happens. Probably nothing.

However, if things have really gone wrong and you do need help, contact the following:

◆ *Mairie* (town hall) for everything local.

◆ *Office de Tourisme/Syndicat d'Initiative* for everything to do with tourism.

◆ *Caisse Primaire d'Assurance Maladie/CPAM* in chief town for the state health insurance.

◆ *Trésor Public* in nearest town for taxes.

◆ Electricity/gas/water see *Yellow Pages*.

◆ The British Embassy in Paris will give you the name of the nearest British consulate for citizenship problems (address in Appendix).

As a last resort if things have not gone according to plan, and especially if you have children, if you really do find yourself without funds go to the local

Caisse Allocations Familiales/CAF (family benefits office) and they may be able to help.

If you have a problem, it's best to go and talk direct to the official concerned, preferably with a French person to help you. If appropriate, present your plausible excuses (not that you didn't understand because you're foreign). They have more discretion than their British counterparts and you might at the very least get let off a penalty.

banque (f)	bank	noir (m)	the black
chèque (m)	cheque	pénalité (f)	penalty
chèque en bois	bounced cheque	relevé bancaire RIB (m)	bank identity slip
chéquier (m)	cheque-book	relevé bancaire de compte	bank statement
chiffre d'affaires (m)	turnover	mensuel	monthly
commerçant (m)	tradesman	taxe (f)	tax
compte (m)	account	hors taxe/HT	without VAT
dégrèvement (m)	reduction	tiers paiement (m)	quarterly
entreprise (f)	business	travailleur independant (m)	self employed
fonctionnaire (m)	official	toutes taxes comprises/TTC	including VAT
imprimé (m)	form	TVA (f)	VAT

Figure 32   Glossary

TIPS FOR MAKING IT PAY

♦ Check all demands for money, including official ones, to see you aren't paying too much.
♦ Pay by the due dates to avoid penalties.
♦ Ask shops you regularly visit for an account.
♦ Go and see the official concerned if you have any queries.

TIP FOR IMPROVING YOUR FRENCH

♦ In France see a TV show or film originally in English and dubbed into French; it's much easier to follow because the actors have to speak more carefully.

11

Not a B&B

If you feel that a B&B alone does not produce a sufficient income, you may want to engage in another activity as well. Or it may be the other way about: you already have another activity and are adding a B&B as a sideline. Either way you will have to work hard to give the guests the impression that they are receiving your undivided attention.

FARMING

This is where *Gîtes de France* came in and farmers still receive special treatment with favourable tax rates and increased grants. Staying on a working farm is immensely popular with both the British and the French and you will have an above-average occupancy rate. As a predominantly agricultural country right up to the 1960s, the French are much nearer their farming roots than other countries. They all like to think of themselves as farming folk. A difficulty for the fastidious Dutch and Americans is that farms do not always look like the idealised pictures. The reality is that it's a muddy and sometimes noisy business. It has to be said that Danish farms are the winners here. Where we stayed the buildings were freshly painted, there were no old cars, and the yard was swept morning and evening after the cows had been in for milking. My children still remember the pigs being born, and it was 25 years ago. Of course, not all farms have animals, at least not the ones you expect. Raising ostriches and llamas still come under the official heading of farming. The type of farm ought to be mentioned in the brochure.

This is one B&B in the country where there's no need for a pool. The surroundings would never be maintained anyway since farmers think gardening is for wimps. And exploit your privileged position by only taking guests for the week, Saturday to Saturday, no messing.

VITICULTURE

Viticulteurs (wine growers) are just as privileged as farmers, but more prestigious. A *chambres d'hôtes* run in conjunction with a vineyard will be very popular with both the French and foreigners. They will naturally expect to taste and buy the wines. It is particularly favoured by companies who run hiking, cycling and car itineraries, though these will be for one-night stays only. For hikers and cyclists, the company usually transports the luggage each day; picnic lunches may be required. *Gîtes de France* have a brochure *Séjours en Vignoble*, or contact one of the many firms who run this type of holiday. If not a *viticuleur* yourself, you could still run a *chambres d'hôtes* in a wine-growing area and make a special feature of visits to vineyards with wine tastings.

There are 12 areas of production:

L'Alsace	La Savoie et le Bugey
Le Beaujolais et le Lyonnais	Le Languedoc et le Roussillon
Le Bordelais	La Provence
La Bourgogne	Le Sud-Ouest
La Champagne	La Vallée de la Loire
Le Jura	La Vallée du Rhône et les Charentes

GITES

One or several *gîtes* are an excellent combination with a B&B. There is a lot of crossover of business both from the B&B to the *gîte* and vice versa. And all without paying for the advertising. However, this won't produce enough guests to fill a *gîte*, and certainly not for several. Some web sites and guides include both B&Bs and *gîtes* but many do not, so you will need to pay for extra advertising.

Gîtes should be away from the main house and have their own private space for sitting out. However some customers may want total privacy and exclusive use of a pool which they won't find when in conjunction with a B&B, so you won't get a premium price. On the other hand, people at a quiet guest house may well have come for a rest and won't be happy to have a group of noisy children from a large *gîte* alongside them. So don't neglect an odd corner for a self-catering studio with a 'no children' policy; this works well as an extra bedroom too or is a good idea if you've already got the maximum number.

I know of one property which is let as a *gîte* during July and August and then as a B&B the rest of the year. The B&B is in a separate building from the house. I have also heard of a couple who had let all of their own house, including the B&B rooms, so they could get away on their own holiday in August, but it was so much work clearing up afterwards that they said 'never again'. Either way you lose potential business to such an extent that I can't see it's worth it.

Gîtes and a B&B go so well together because the work for both is so similar. The bookings, the cleaning, the laundry, the being on hand for arrivals are common to both. You can provide linen, where absent owners find this difficult. If you have a *table d'hote* you can provide dinner. We found the *gîte* tenants usually took dinner at least once during their stay, and invariably came to the barbecues. One couple even had dinner every night. Some *gîte* owners offer dinner on the first night as an inducement; this wouldn't be difficult for you.

ACTIVITY HOLIDAYS

These are basically either sporting, or acquiring skills.

If you are offering the sport yourself, then you **must** be qualified in that speciality and possess all the right certificates. You need to decide whether these activities are an option for the guests generally, or a specialised week dedicated solely to that sport. For the former, you would mention it in your general advertising. For the latter you would have to advertise in the relevant sports magazines. You could, of course, offer the sport generally in the high season, with specialized weeks out of season. **Watch the capital expenditure.**

Classes in languages, regional cookery, art, music, and many crafts can be run in conjunction with a B&B. There are many of them, so there is stiff competition. Most are run as a whole week's course, and are often held in the mid-season months. Really you need to be an experienced teacher of the subject concerned to give good value to the participants.

All activity holidays have some organising problems in common:

1. Which language? If in English, it excludes everyone else. It makes proceedings very slow if everything has to be said twice.

2. Many people will come as singles, so are there enough bedrooms or will they share?

3. A couple may have one partner who doesn't want to take part in the activity. What are they to do with their time?

4. Is it absolutely clear who provides the equipment and appropriate clothing? If someone arrives missing some items what will you do?

5. What if there are cancellations? What if only two people book? Would the activity still go ahead?

6. For outdoor activities what provision is there for bad weather?

7. If applicable: what about transport to the activity? What about transport for the usual free choice day?

8. Many activities held on the premises will need a specially designated room. As a workshop is the lighting adequate? For dance and gymnastics is the floor suitable? For music are the acoustics alright? For either of the latter do they need a good piano? And for everyone is the heating adequate? For cookery I assume you will use your own kitchen, so is it large enough?

9. What about laundry?

10. The general web sites and brochures will not produce enough customers for special activities, so where will you advertise?

11. What will you do in the weeks when there is no activity scheduled? To run it as a conventional B&B would necessitate an additional set of advertising.

12. Are you absolutely confident it will pay?

Here are two case studies (*Fig. 33*) showing two completely different ways of running art classes.

Case **A** is more of a hostel than a B&B and it has functioned well for many years.

Case **B** has only just started, so one cannot say how well it will do. I am concerned that they are starting with such a lot of debt and they both have taken on a heavy work load. They could find themselves working 70 hours a week, which is not what they came to France for. I'm sure they will make changes – we all do – and will make it into a success.

Much, much easier than organising activities yourself is using other people's expertise. If you were ever keen on a sport, or better still achieved some success, then capitalise on this and locate the B&B accordingly. Feature the local facilities prominently in your advertising. Let someone else provide the expertise, location, materials and insurance.

OTHER POSSIBILITIES

A *ferme auberge* (country restaurant) often has a *chambre d'hôte* as well which is ideal for customers. The menu **has** to include home-produced meat

	A	**B**
Previous career	Art teacher and practising artist	Commercial artist, no teaching experience
Reason for change	Retirement	On reaching 40 wanted to get away from 70-hour week
Family	Wife, no children still at home	Wife, 2 young children at private school
Property	Picturesque isolated stone farm buildings	1960's luxury stone-clad villa in elegant suburb of Mediterranean resort
Accommodation	Sleeps 24 in 11 bedrooms in farm buildings round a courtyard	Sleeps 8: 2 bedrooms in house, 2 in guest house, all with private patio
Bathrooms	Communal bathrooms	En-suite to each room
Grounds	Extensive former fields, good views, no pool	2-acre beautifully kept garden with 2 swimming pools
In wet weather	Barn	No provision
Art staff	1 other art teacher	He does all the teaching
Classes	No formal classes; students invited to put work up in barn for daily crit	Students taken to selected site every day in people carrier
Housekeeping	Wife supervises students who have to do a day's housekeeping + cooking every other day	Wife does all housekeeping plus all meals for full board
Advertising	Via art schools	Glossy brochure and web site
Period available	Summer only due to lack of heating	All year due to climate and central heating
Cost of property	Bought cheaply for cash	Very expensive, with mortgage
Renovation	Adding partitions, stairs, basic bathrooms, windows	En-suite bathrooms, +large amount on house as had not been well maintained
Cost of course and full board	Very cheap, aimed at all ages	Expensive, aimed at mature clients

Figure 33   Two case studies of very different art classes

to justify the name and there have been some prosecutions recently for people operating under false pretences. Naturally this is going to be a farm.

Chalets and camp sites could also have some B&Bs, usually making use of an old house already on the site.

If you have real catering experience and a big enough suitable room how about incorporating weddings and functions generally? Some guests will want to stay one or more nights. You would also need a full restaurant license. The trouble with weddings is that most of them are in the summer. A B&B by itself does not have enough rooms for seminars as they are generally made up of single people, unless you add a *gîte* or two. There are many possibilities.

For these kind of developments you should discuss them first with all the interested parties i.e. the *Comité Départemental de Tourisme*, the *Direction Départementale de l'Equipement*, and the water and electricity companies because there may be constraints you don't know about. They are large businesses requiring plenty of capital and administrative skill to run profitably. Since a B&B is so labour intensive are you sure you will have the time and energy?

NOT A *CHAMBRES D'HOTES*

Are you quite sure you want to be a *chambres d'hôtes* at all? There are other interesting possibilities. *Gîtes de France* have the following categories:

Gîtes Panda	(children)
Gîtes d'Enfants	(children)
Gîtes d'Etape et de Séjour	(hostels and large gîtes)
Séjours à la Neige	(skiing)
Séjours Equestres	(riding)
Séjours Pêche	(fishing)
Séjours Vignoble	(vineyards)

They are all more hostels than B&Bs, but might suit your particular property and interests. To find out more, the best thing is to stay in one.

TIPS FOR MAKING IT PAY

◆ Advertise to reach the target customers.

◆ Do not take on anything for which you don't have the experience.

◆ Do not have too many special activities or expend too much capital until you are sure it is profitable.

◆ Have a back-up plan for when things go wrong.

◆ Have a party on the last night so that it's remembered as an enjoyable week that will be recommended to friends.

TIP FOR IMPROVING YOUR FRENCH

◆ In France join an art or craft class at a club or institute to practise conversation. The Tourist Office will probably have a list.

12

Organising the Publicity

To make money, it is necessary to advertise **a lot**. Repeat bookings, word of mouth, friends and relatives from the UK, passing trade: none of these produce nearly enough customers. If there are five bedrooms, that's $5 \times 365 = 1,825$ nights a year and it takes a lot of effort even to fill half. You've **got** to fill the rooms, as there's no other way for your investment to pay off. To make full use of three or more bedrooms in the first year, it will probably take 25 per cent of your gross income, for the next few years 10 per cent, and should drop to 5 per cent when the business is established. In contrast, for one or two bedrooms it is best to limit the advertising cost to the absolute minimum, possibly even none at all. There's been a revolution in advertising and booking in the tourist trade in the last ten years – it's called the World Wide Web and it looks set to make further advances, so you need to join in. **Always** ask your guests where they found your name to judge the value of each outlet. Try a new one every year, but unfortunately you'll find it is possible for an advertisement not to produce a single response.

THE ORGANISATIONS

Becoming a member

It is not compulsory to join an organisation but as a newcomer I strongly recommend it, and in fact there's nothing to stop you joining more than one. The following are all sponsored by the government who spend a lot on promoting tourism, but none are an exact equivalent of the British Tourist Boards. There is usually a *droit d'entré* (entry fee), always an annual *cotisation* (subscription) and a system of inspection. In return you get an entry in their guide book and on their web page, plus a lot of help if you want it and access to grants. They do however produce the write-ups on your property without you getting the chance of correcting the proofs. Breakfast must always be included in the price but they do all recognise that it's your own personal option as to whether you want to provide dinners or not.

As soon as your premises appear in one of these organisation's books you will begin to receive invitations to feature in the commercial guides, and if you don't belong to any the tourist offices won't list you. Naturally some proprietors will reckon they don't need any help.

Gîtes de France

Maison des Gîtes de France et du Tourisme Vert,
59 rue St-Lazare,
75439 Paris, France.
01 49 70 75 75
www.gites-de-france.com

Founded more than 50 years ago, this is the largest organisation with over 10,000 B&B members, plus *gîtes*, hostels, *fermes auberges* and chalets, and they also advise foreign governments on promoting rural tourism. So it's a big organisation with a well known logo. However, their remit is the countryside so members **have** to be in the country or a village: towns are out and so are housing estates. Several commercial publishers in France and other countries use their data base, though the clients using their own guide books will be mostly French.

Though they don't like one bedroom premises their average number of bedrooms is only 2.5, so the target membership is really people looking for a second income. There is a large showroom at their headquarters in Paris but the organisation is run independently by the 95 *départements*. Each has a paid staff and a committee of volunteers drawn from members; they set the fees, make the inspections and to a large extent make up their own rules. They will arrive for an inspection with up to seven people, all the bedrooms must be ready to let and they usually ask for a sample breakfast to be set out, although they don't actually eat it. Some of their various demands can seem trivial, such as the corn flakes should have been decanted into containers or the bedspreads are not good enough, and they are generally prejudiced against modern furniture in B&Bs. With so many foreigners now running B&B's some ability to speak French is required. About one third of members have a table d'hôte.

There is a bible-size guide of all B&B's without photos, together with separate regional and *département* booklets. Then there is the 'Chambres d'Hôtes Prestige' for three and four *épis* members at an extra charge, and several specialist booklets such as 'Gîtes de Neige' which are by invitation if appropriate. Most *départements* run an optional booking service and there is a same-night telephone booking line '*Allo Chambres d'Hôtes*', on 0891 16 22 22. For members there is a quarterly magazine in French – in fact the organisation is run entirely in French though the web page does have an English version.

Most branches have an annual meeting followed by a rather jolly meal where the real business takes place. You can make friends with other owners and exchange your horror stories: 'there was this couple who were cooking a meal in their bedroom on a camping gas stove . . .'. Even though they normally expect you to fill in endless surveys I would recommend joining.

Clévacances

Fédération National des Locations de France Clévacances
54 boulevard de l'Embouchure,
31022 Toulouse, France.
05 61 13 55 66
www.clevacances.com

The numbers of *gîtes* and B&Bs rose enormously in the 1980s and 1990s, with many of them quite unregulated, so the government founded this particular organisation to complement *Gîtes de France*. Once again, it has a national federation and is run independently by the *départements*, but uses local tourist offices for all the legwork involved in inspections and advice. Thus the fees are smaller but there is less back up. They accept premises in towns and cities, including Paris, housing estates and even if only one bedroom in a flat (not uncommon in Paris). Their guide book is not very widely distributed and so does not produce so many bookings, but clients can book online using the web site. Go to your tourist office for information.

Fleurs de Soleil

52 avenue Thermal
03200 Vichy, France
www.fleurs-soleil.tm.fr

Part of the *Association des Maisons d'Amis en France*, this was founded in 1997 by a group of proprietors who believed that the above organisations were too big and too impersonal, but does not check that B&B's are actually in the homes of owners or verify that the owners are not hidden professionals. Containing over 400 premises, all of these are visited and all locations and types of building can be considered. Their guide book is one of the series published by Samedi-Midi (see under Bed & Breakfast Guides).

Accueil Paysan

Fédération Nationale Accueil Paysan,
MIN-117 rue des Alliés
38030 Grenoble, France.
04 76 43 44 83
www.accueil-paysan.com

Founded in 1987 and strictly for working farmers only, clients are guaranteed their dream holiday on a genuine farm. They have over 600 members and are linked to similar associations abroad where they will arrange exchange visits. There is no grading and naturally they strongly promote *tables d'hôtes* using home produce. The *Guide Accueil Paysan* is obtainable from the above address only.

Hôtes Qualité Paris

www.hotesqualiteparis.fr

This is a grouping of three separate organisations for the purpose of promoting B&B accommodation in Paris and is funded by the mayor. Each is run quite independently. Those B&Bs accepted and given the 'Hôtes Qualité' label will get assistance, grants and publicity. I really wouldn't try and go it alone in Paris.

1. Fleurs de Soleil
See above.

2. 2BINPARIS
See under Bed & Breakfast Guides – a commercial company with 107 B&Bs in Paris.

3. *Association Française* B&B in France
See in Bed & Breakfast Guides under Thomas Cook – a commercial company with 68 B&Bs in Paris.

Grading

Both *Gîtes de France* and *Clévacances* award all their members one to four stars or *épis* (ears of corn) for the former and *clés* (keys) for the latter; the others do not have their own grading system. The classifications matter to the public and grades one and two are not popular. An upgrade from two to three can increase bookings fourfold. Even more relevant is that many of the commercial guides use these grades when selecting premises for their publications, and generally they are not interested in one or two pips.

If you are only awarded two *épis/clés* it might not be worth joining yet and asking what improvements are needed to obtain a grade three. Perhaps the tourist office can help with the negotiations. Upgrading from three to four is more difficult. If the coveted grade four is beyond you, decide whether it really is worth spending any more or would it be better to settle for being an excellent grade three. The disadvantage of upgrading later is that publishers and others may not notice.

Unfortunately there are criticisms of the standards as they are not uniform throughout the country and there are no yearly incognito visits to see that they are maintained. Another problem area is that *Gîtes de France* expect the interiors to be in traditional French style and this is a very subjective judgement.

THE WEB

Some proprietors **only** advertise on the web and receive 80 per cent of their bookings that way, but as most e-mails arrive in working hours this means they are largely from people at work. However, staying in a *chambre d'hôte* is very much an older person's choice, so perhaps it would pay to cast your net wider. In fact the web has not caught on so much in France. People are still somewhat cautious, and some will even have seen you on the web but will still phone to make their booking. A valid reason for such caution is that if you don't belong to any organisation then your B&B will not have been visited and graded.

Commercial organisations that make the bookings themselves will have a site with enough information for clients to make their own choice and book. The reservation is then sent to you by email and you are saved a lot of administration time and effort.

If you are taking bookings yourself it is necessary either to join an organisation, all of which have a site with contact information and other details of your property, or to pay a commercial host site, where many will have a link to your own web site. There are many free sites of almost nil value for bookings, but they will give extra links to your page and the more links you have the better your chances of a good listing on search engines.

It is not essential to have your own web page but it's becoming more and more popular with owners and the public. Unless you are really confident, setting it up yourself will be time consuming and will not produce the best result. Better pay an experienced hand, but make a careful choice as there are cowboys about. Expect to pay about €750. Your site is in fact your brochure, and for some owners the only brochure, so it should contain all the information as before with the addition of availability and an e-mail booking form. This availability information will need updating regularly. There will also be a monthly charge for the server where you place your site, and it needs to be in place at least three months before you open for business.

It's a volatile market but here are some host sites which can provide links to your page:

www.bvdirect.co.uk
www.2binparis.com
www.cheznous.com
www.frenchconnections.co.uk
www.karenbrown.com
www.ourinns.org
www.petitfute.com
www.pour-les-vacances.com
www.vacancesfrance.com
www.visitfrance.co.uk

BED & BREAKFAST GUIDES

Get maximum benefit

There are many of these but only about a dozen that have a large enough distribution to be effective, with new ones coming and going frequently. Visit the French Tourist Office in Piccadilly for a good selection. Be cautious before committing any fees because it has been known for publishers to make their income from selling the advertising space and not from selling the book, with their expert supposed to have visited a property actually staying in another hotel. However, if the entry is free there's unlikely to be anything to lose. Guides that are distributed free of charge are only used in the first year, with those paid for maybe kept for up to three years, so the business builds up year by year. Our extreme case was someone using a six year old edition! Have a good spread of nationalities. Be aware that those guides promising a rigorous selection may well throw you out on receipt of a second complaint, whether it is valid or not.

Some guides write the entry themselves and you will not get a chance to correct the proofs, so there will sometimes be mistakes. Others will have the proprietor do it and send you a proof. Unfortunately this work usually has to be done right in the middle of high season, so it's as well to have thought out your policy earlier because it is essential not to miss the deadline. After the photograph it's the wording in bold print that grabs attention.

Follow these tips for preparing your own entry:

1. Push the establishment's key features.

2. Avoid flowery language and keep to the facts.

3. Be truthful and don't exaggerate.

4. Mention the warm welcome and any features that are 'new this year'.

5. Be brief in describing the locality and concentrate on the property.

6. Give a contact name.

A selection of guides

Organisation	Name of Guide	Address	Nationality
Alistair Sawday	French Bed & Breakfast	The Old Farmyard Yanley Lane Long Ashton Bristol BS41 9LR 01275 395430 www.sawdays.co.uk	British (also sold in the US)

This was the first of their many guides. All premises are visited initially (not all are selected) and there are incognito check ups. There is a fee and they write the half page entry. Updated every two years.

| Automobile Association Lifestyle Guides | Bed & Breakfast in France | – | | British |

The well known association, they obtain your name from *Gîtes de France* and you will be invited to appear in their publication.

| Chez Nous | France | Spring Mill Earby, Barnoldswick Lancashire BB94 0AA 0870 197 1000 www.cheznous.com | British |

Primarily for gîtes with over 3,000 properties listed but produces good results for B&Bs as well. At £418 for ⅛ page and £678 for ¼ page + VAT this is the most expensive of all. It's worth it when there is a gîte as well as the B&B because both are included in the same advertisement and in this case a ¼ page is best. The large page format ensures a good display in bookshops. The guide is not sent abroad and premises are not visited.

| Filipacchi | 150 Chambres d'Hôtes & Hotels de Charme | (part of Hachette) | French (also sold in the US) |

Just one of the titles from an indefatigable couple who visit every establishment themselves.

| Hachette Tourisme | (specialist titles) | Hachette Editions 43 quai Grenelle 75015 Paris 01 43 92 30 00 | French |

France's largest publisher. Titles: '*Chambres d'Hôtes Secrèts*', 300 B&Bs and small hotels chosen for their interest as buildings; '*Chambres d'Hôtes au Château*', 100 examples; '*Chambres d'Hôtes Insolites*', 120 unusual B&Bs and hotels. Plus others, all entries selected by experts.

| Hotels Abroad | Hotels Abroad | 5 Worlds End Lane Orpington Kent BR6 6AA 0845 330 2500 www.hotelsabroad.com | British |

Surprisingly they do include some B&Bs. It's really aimed at travellers so stays will mostly be one night and you need to be easily accessible. They do the booking.

| Karen Brown | Karen Brown's France B&B | PO Box 70 San Mateo California 94401 www.karenbrown.com | USA |

In association with the French guide '*Relais et Châteaux*' so you need to be first rate. All the hype that comes with an American company.

| Michelin | Charming Places France | www.michelin.co.uk | Worldwide |

Their Guide is subtitled '1000 Charming Hotels & Guesthouses'. To be considered a guesthouse there needs to be at least three bedrooms. Worldwide distribution. Contact: Librairie Ariane, 20 rue Cap. Dreyfus, 35000 Rennes; tel 02 99 79 68 47.

| Le Petit Futé | Petit Futé Bed & Breakfast | rue Maupertus 35170 Bruz, France 02 99 059 050 www.petitfute.com | French |

A large publishing house with over 400 tourist titles and 700 B&Bs in this volume. They do not visit. A classified advertisement placed on their web site will appear in five minutes. Also published in the UK, Germany and Italy.

| Rivages | Maisons d'Hôtes De Charme France | 106 bd Saint-Germain 75006 Paris, France 01 44 41 39 90 www.guidesdecharme. com | French |

The most upmarket and the best value because there is no fee. But the selection is very rigorous and independent of any other organisation. In the country is preferred and it doesn't have to be a chateau or mansion, as interesting houses are accepted too. Self-catering suites can also be mentioned. There are over 700 properties with half a page each; they write the entry and you will receive a proof to check the facts. There are also incognito check ups. Part of the large publishing house Payot & Rivages, it is also published in English, German and Italian.

Routard	Nos Meilleures Chambres d'Hôtes en France	www.routard.com (send an email from the site)	French

Part of the publisher Hachette, with dozens more guides covering many activities and most parts of the world.

Samedi Midi Créations	(specialist titles)	18 rue d'Enghein 89002 Lyon, France 04 78 37 56 46 www.samedimidi.com	French

Small publishers of many guides themed by area, by geography, by sports available, by courses available, etc. Also publishes the guide for the association *'Fleurs de Soleil'*. They inspect and make incognito visits.

Thomas Cook	Bed & Breakfast France	Bed & Breakfast France PO Box 47085 London SW18 9AB 0871 781 0834 www.bedbreak.com	Br/Fr

The travel pioneer Thomas Cook produces this guide in association with the company Bed & Breakfast France. Their associated French company makes the visits and has their own grading system of 'suns', but they also take the bookings (in English if required). About 750 premises. Member of *'Hôtes Qualité Paris'*.

MAGAZINES, NEWSPAPERS, DIRECTORIES

The magazines *France*, *The Lady* and *The Oldie* have all produced good results (for addresses see Appendix B). You can either have a classified or a larger entry. They do have rather a short shelf life, but are useful if you have missed the autumn deadlines for the main guides.

In-house and specialist magazines can be used, nothing lost if they are free, but they do have a small readership and even smaller number of people just happening to be planning a trip to France and staying in a B&B.

The daily newspapers and their travel supplements are expensive and have the shortest shelf life of all, but try a classified entry and see if it works.

You may be solicited to appear in various trade directories, I doubt if it's worth it. And that goes for paying for an entry in the *Yellow Pages* too, because *chambres d'hôtes* are put under *gîtes* and no one thinks of looking there.

PHOTOGRAPHS

Customers will have chosen the area and price before searching for a particular establishment. Once they start to look at advertisements, it's the photograph that makes the greatest impact. Employ a professional if possible; the cost will be recovered in extra bookings. But if taking them yourself, here are some tips:

1. Choose the time of day when the view is in full sunlight and the sky is blue.

2. Avoid winter when the leaves are off the trees.

3. If you have a pool a picture is essential.

4. Take pictures of any other attractive features of the property such as the garden, beamed interiors, large fireplace.

5. Place something on the bed such as books, magazines, pile of towels or a peignoir.

6. Open shutters, close windows, and remove all clutter.

7. Add a garden table and chairs. Place some fruit, flowers or tray of drinks on the table.

8. Flowers are always winners. Add hanging baskets, window-boxes or large pots with flowers. Take a view of the property with sunflowers, wisteria or blossom if possible.

9. Experiment with climbing up a ladder. A particularly good idea for interior views.

10. Don't include people, but animals are acceptable.

Always keep the publicity material and photos handy; you never know when there might be an opening.

BROCHURE AND STATIONERY

For one or two bedrooms, do you really need a brochure? An elegant visiting card is more sophisticated than a leaflet on thin paper. Or have a card of the format ⅓ of an A4 sheet. This fits neatly into a standard envelope and would contain just the name, address, possibly a map, and a space for writing in the price by hand.

With several bedrooms, a well designed brochure is **essential**. It will pay to have it professionally designed, but it won't pay for each copy to cost too much. If they cost more than £1 each you will be inhibited from distributing them freely. They either need to be professionally printed, or can you produce a good job with a desk-top printer?

Checklist of the information that should be included:

Front page
1. Drawing or photo of the building or an interesting part of it.

2. Name of establishment.

3. What you do:
    i.e. Chambres d'Hôtes/Bed & Breakfast
    or Maison d'Hôtes/Country Guest House
    (+Table d'Hôte).

4. Name of town, village or region + 'France'.

5. Logo if you belong to an association.

Interior

6. A few words of description of your establishment (don't be too long winded), include number of bedrooms and 'all rooms with en-suite bathroom'.

7. Don't be shy about mentioning a small detail that could put you ahead of the competition, such as: Champagne aperitif before dinner on Saturdays, fresh flowers in the bedroom, a branded special soap. It gives a very good impression.

8. Where appropriate mention dinners and lunches and show a sample menu, or give distance to nearest restaurant.

9. Describe the swimming pool and other amenities, preferably with pictures.

10. Brief description of places to visit and sports facilities nearby.

11. A few items of essential information such as: policies on children/animals/smoking/and dates of closure.

12. Preferably have pictures of a bedroom and the dining-room.

13. Mention any other activities such as '*gîtes*' or 'working farm'.

14. Mention any other languages you speak.

Last page

15. Thumbnail diagram of France with a dot to show where you are.

16. Location map of the immediate vicinity and the nearest village. It's the last five miles that really matter, Michelin will cope with the rest.

17. The words 'For further information contact':
    Name of proprietor
    Full address, phone/fax, email and web.

To get all the above on, the usual format is an A4 sheet folded in three. The brochure should either be in French and English, plus any other language of course, or have a separate one for each (watch the cost). If in both languages, the English can be just a brief translation. The translation into French **must** be done by a French national; if you don't know anyone ask the tourist office. You will see I have suggested 'country guest house' as a possible alternative to 'bed & breakfast', which may be a better translation if you have several bedrooms with *table d'hôte*. It's best to have the price list on a separate sheet which is inserted into the folded brochure, then it can be changed every year. Ask a friend to look over the brochure layout before having 300 printed; it's amazing what can get left out.

You will also need headed writing paper, set up on the computer of course, and visiting cards. Ideally there should be a uniformity of style between these and the brochure because they will often be sent out together. Sooner or later you will be solicited to have a photo of your place on a postcard, and these are a good promotional idea.

OUTDOOR SIGNS

It's a big complaint of customers that B&Bs are not well-signposted. When clients get lost on a hot day after a long drive, they arrive cross, and that's not a good start. You will have noticed a somewhat more relaxed attitude to signs in France compared to the UK. You need something in the centre of your village, and at every turning until your establishment is reached. By right you can have a sign 300 metres away from your entrance in both directions. Standard signs are available from road sign manufacturers; ask at the *Direction Départementale de l'Equipement* for an address as they are ordering all the time. Or you may prefer something more individual with your name on; get quotes from a firm listed under *Signalisation* in the Yellow Pages.

Then you need a sign at your entrance, and its size depends on how commercial you want to be: large if you want to attract passing trade, discreet otherwise. Both *Gîtes de France* and *Clévacances* **insist** that members display their logo at the entrance. **Never** have a home-made sign, it looks very amateurish. Unfortunately, painted signs on wood don't last beyond a couple of years unless protected by an overhanging roof.

Don't put up a sign saying *complet* (full), because surely you want people to come to the front door and see what a nice place it is. However, a sign saying *ouvert* (open) is a good idea in winter (if that is the case).

The above applies to an individual house where you want to make your presence felt. Other proprietors will want to remain exclusive or perhaps will only let one room in a city flat and will rely solely on advance bookings and recommendations. In these situations just have a small plate at the entrance or front door with enough information to convince customers they have arrived at the right address.

EXPLOIT OTHER POSSIBILITIES

There are a number of ways to advertise for free. Don't neglect them.

First is your tourist office. Keep it supplied with brochures, and keep in touch with the personnel to remind them of your existence. You can also leave brochures in all the other centres in your *département* if you think it worth it. But in another *département* they either won't be accepted or a fee will be required which is unlikely to be worthwhile.

Next comes leaving a stack of visiting cards with all other likely looking establishments: restaurants, estate agents, tourist shops, sports clubs. Hotels are likely to be a bit sniffy about a B&B, because they think we don't have proper chefs and don't pay taxes.

Join some clubs to get known; there is a lot of local business to be picked up. Also get to know all the other *chambres d'hôtes* owners in the vicinity so that you can pass on customers between you when full.

One day I saw a name and the words '*chambres d'hôtes*' signwritten on the door of a 4WD. I mentally saluted that owner as being very businesslike. The moral is to keep an eye open for possibilities.

REPEAT BUSINESS AND RECOMMENDATIONS

One always hopes that guests will recommend you and come back themselves another time – it's very satisfying. And as your name gets known it means you can advertise less. But don't expect too much; it doesn't happen often enough to fill the rooms, and anyway we are all very restless these days. We don't often go back to the same place.

Our repeat business grew year by year, but many were not strictly holidaymakers. They were friends or relatives of people living nearby, attending local sporting events, or househunting/renovating/moving in.

You could send a 'thank you' note after guests leave, a Christmas card to the British, or a New Year's card to the French; and even include a photo taken during their stay: only if they're people you want back of course. Don't omit the people who enquired but didn't come. But just be a little cautious who you contact afterwards; it isn't always welcome. One proprietor returned a pair of black lace knickers to the address given, only to receive them back again with a note: 'These are not mine'.

BUSINESS NAME

The business name needs careful thought. Within a village there will be a road name and a number exactly the same as in the UK, so you need a name for the enterprise. Have a sign made and hung at right angles to the street. In the country the situation differs. There are **no road names**, only road numbers and it does make addresses difficult to find. Instead there is the *lieu-dit* (literally 'place called'), which featured on the deeds. This is the official name of the land, not the house. If there are ten houses on the same parcel of land, they all have the same name.

Since the *lieu-dit* is the official name, it cannot be changed; but you can use any name you like for business purposes. Unless the property is a local landmark such as a château, or a mill, there are advantages in choosing a suitable business name. Looking far ahead to when you retire, you have either got something more to put in the basket of goodies when you sell as a going concern, or you take the sign down and are free of people knocking on the door for the next five years and wanting a bed for the night. The name would go above the *lieu-dit* as the address.

Tips for choosing a business name:

1. With the help of a French speaker choose a dozen possibles.

2. Consider using the name of your village or something relating to its history, and a feature of the area could be used as a logo.

3. Avoid names that are difficult to pronounce in French or English.

4. Do not include any words in English.

5. Long names are difficult to fit on a sign.

6. Choose an unusual word or the search engines will report dozens of examples.

7. Many lists are in alphabetical order, so you should be near the beginning.

8. Consult another French person to double check that the one chosen is suitable. You don't want to be mistaken for a retirement home or religious institution.

To tie it all together, you now need a logo; nothing fancy, just the name always in the same type face. It should be the same on everything: outdoor signs, brochure, letter head, visiting cards. Add a little symbol such as a feature of the building, tree, bird or animal only if you are confident to do it. Then scan it into the computer and use it on everything.

CHEQUES VACANCES

This is a scheme on the lines of luncheon vouchers, but is for holidays, restaurants and some leisure activities. They are given to employees by large French companies. The client pays with the vouchers and you claim the money back from the organisation. You have to be a member, but as it costs nothing you might as well. They only take 1 per cent commission. Members get a classified entry in the guide book and on the web site, and in the latter with a useful location map. Contact *Agence Nationale pour les Chèques-Vacances* at www.ancv.com

THE FIRST YEAR

This is the most difficult of all, and if the business is sparse, it is very discouraging. Firstly: were you able to get into any guides the previous autumn? If a photo of the outside was impossible, then perhaps one of a bedroom. If you did not achieve that, then it will have to be a web page or magazines or newspapers which have later publishing dates. Whatever the method, it **must** be published by mid-January if you are to have any sort of season at all. Naturally you will be frantically busy getting the place ready, but speed and effort are essential. Do not put up a sign and sit back and **wait** for the business to take off – they can't see the sign in Wigan. How about having a *vin d'honneur* (an open day with wine and nibbles) the day before you open? They are very common and any occasion will do, so print an invitation card and ask **everyone** you can think of to come. It's a good publicity opportunity that won't come again. (*For a glossary of publicity terms, see Fig. 34.*)

agenda (m)	diary	droit d'entrée (m)	enrolment fee
annonce (f)	advertisment	épi (m)	ear of corn
petite annonce (f)	classified ad	guide (f)	guide
bôite aux lettres (f)	letter box	panneau (m)	outdoor sign
brochure (f)	brochure	*Pages Jaunes* (f)	*Yellow Pages*
carte (f)	map	rendez-vous (m)	appointment
carte de visite (f)	visiting card	renseignements (m)	information
coordonnées (f)	address, etc.	réunion (f)	meeting
cotisation (f)	subscription	syndicat d'initiative (m)	tourist office
dépliant (m)	leaflet		

Figure 34   Glossary

TIPS FOR MAKING IT PAY

- Advertise a lot.
- Plan your advertising early.
- Advertise to attract different nationalities.

TIP FOR IMPROVING YOUR FRENCH

- Write a business letter in French.

13

Looking After the Staff

YOURSELVES

Imagine yourself in the guests' place for a moment. They get out of their carriage to find a warm welcome, the beds made, the fires lit, and a meal will shortly be put on the table; and all without any effort on their part. Could be a scene from a costume drama set a hundred years ago, couldn't it? I'm not saying that they are the nobs and you are the servants; we're all egalitarian now. But what you are really offering is a house with servants. For one night or fourteen nights, the guests' expectation is that they have paid to be waited on. Though one big difference between now and then is that now you own the house, not them, and this alters the balance considerably. Let us just say that nowadays 'looked after' can be substituted for 'waited on'. To give the feel of how this situation originated, I have included 'Mrs Beeton's Book of Household Management' in the book list in the Appendix; not for the recipes, but do read the section on servants.

In very grand houses there was a servant for everything, even a 'boots'. I'm glad we don't polish trainers, or we'd be doing that too. As it is, the one or two or three of you are chambermaid, cleaner, cook, washer-upper, gardener, receptionist, computer techie, financial manager, advertising manager, secretary, purchasing officer, upholsterer, laundry maid, plumber, electrician, waiter, painter and decorator – to name only a few. We ran an ambulance service once, too, when a guest had to go to hospital at 4am.

What are the hours? Well, the latest any guests arrived back at night was 5am (they had been to a wedding), and the earliest any guests left in the morning was 5am (to avoid the heat and traffic on a long journey). Fortunately these events were exceptional, and you aren't expected to be around. But someone does need to be around between 7am and 11pm; if one of the partners is a lark and the other an owl then the hours can be staggered to suit. You should be able to get a reasonable break in the middle of the day, though between 13.30 and 14.00 is a favourite time for the French to phone. I hope I've not presented too daunting a picture, because the above only applies to the high season. Mid-season will mostly be easier, unless you have a group. And October to Easter you'll be lucky to have many guests at all, unless you're a ski resort. Not that you can rest. There's everything to be got ready for next season, but at least you can work at your own pace.

For holidays, the best months to go away are November and December, but it's not ideal to leave such a public sort of place as a B&B empty while you go away, as all sorts of people will generally come to the door. Can you prevail on someone to house-sit? In January and February there will be a lot of enquiries and bookings, though it's so much easier now that emails can be picked up wherever you are; unfortunately, you may feel you are never on holiday.

You will acclimatise much more quickly to living abroad by wholly accepting all things French than by constantly popping 'home' for the things you can't do without. Have a French car, use a French dentist, and you will soon find there's a French equivalent for 90 per cent of your favourite British foods.

RELATIVES AND FRIENDS

They'll all want to visit in the first year. You won't be too busy (except with the DIY), so that's not a problem. After that you'll have to make some rules if they're not to fill the guest rooms in high season. You could designate a 'family week' in which you don't accept any visitors and can then devote your full time to the family. The last week of August would be a good choice as it's not as popular as the first three weeks. Or for friends generally you could say that if they come in high season they have to pay full rate, and you won't be able to spare them any time. But if they come out of season you'll have more time and there will be no charge. I would be very cautious if anyone says they will come as a 'working party'. It will cost **at least** £30 a week to feed them.

CHILDREN

If you have dependent children the finances of the business must be taken very seriously. Few B&Bs produce a family size income. So either the business must be expanded beyond just a B&B, or one of the parents must take an outside job. The latter leaves only one person to look after the children and run the B&B as well. Up to three rooms will be manageable; for more rooms you'll only cope if you don't do dinners or you have plenty of help. Of course children of ten and over should make excellent slave labour in the summer.

HELP IN THE HOUSE

It won't be long before you want to employ a *femme de ménage* (cleaning lady), as there's so much to do. For your own part of the house you can use the simple system of *Cheque Emploi Service Universal/CESU*, which consists of paying the person via an official cheque and all the social security payments will be dealt with automatically. You must pay the minimum wage at the very least, which can be found on www.cesu.urssaf.fr. This is for private household tasks only, but it's likely your own premises will receive scant attention otherwise. A business with less than five employees can also use a version of the above scheme; your bank will set this up for you.

In the early years and given that a B&B is seasonal you may want to find some paid employment for the winter. I'm afraid this will be very difficult unless you have a special skill to offer, and poor French will be held against you. You could ask at the *mairie* about any organisations offering a home help service that you could join and this will be paid employment.

How do you find your reliable, clean, hardworking, honest treasure? With difficulty is the answer. Ask other ex-pats, or that fount of local gossip: your hairdresser. At the interview, the following points need to be covered:

◆ Which days to come. If you need them on Saturday this is the **first** thing to establish.

◆ The pay.

◆ The hours. The French do not normally work between 12.00 and 14.00 hours.

◆ Will they be taking off for their own holiday in July or August? This is **crucial. Will they work over the August 15th holiday?**

◆ If there are young children, what arrangements will be made for them?

◆ You could always ask if they would be willing to take the ironing home with them (only if they have a car of course).

◆ It's only fair to say if the job is temporary, i.e. finishing at the end of September.

◆ Ask for at least two references, from other ex-pats if possible, then be sure to follow them up.

I expect you will be asked for a bit more than the minimum wage for a regular morning cleaning person. Confirm all the above in writing, presumably in French (you'll have to do your best). If they are young and still at school, be very, very, wary if you are intending to pay them. Has their mother taught them how to make a bed or clean a bathroom? If in any doubt, the best thing is to say they can come for a trial period, though if it doesn't work out, you can be in a real fix, with the season started, and no help. One quirk of the indigenous population is that their stomachs all rumble at precisely midday. In fact you've got to be a long way out in the country to be out of earshot of the hooters that sound off at this hour. Midday is sacrosanct as the lunch hour. This is not very convenient when the guests have ignored your requirement to leave by 10am, and are still around at 11. How are you ever to get the rooms done?

The number of days a cleaning person needs to come will depend on how often the rooms are serviced. You will find the weekends particularly busy. Although you are not a *gîte* with a fixed changeover day of Saturday, you will find that many guests do choose to arrive on this day, and then of course no one wants to work on Sundays.

You can use their first name for a cleaning person, but for other tradesmen use their surname at least at first; and you only shake hands the first time you meet, not every day. My cleaning lady said I was much too polite, she never got 'please' and 'thank you' when working in a hotel. I kept to the British way.

If you have imported friends or relatives from the UK to help out, where are they going to sleep? They certainly can't have one of the guest rooms, and it can't be a sofa for six weeks or more. Failing any room in the house, and since it's summer, the options are: a caravan, a summer house, or a minimum conversion in an ancillary building. With all of these, the sanitary arrangements will be difficult. Even though it's warm, there can be terrific storms with ten minutes of torrential rain, so camping isn't really an option for someone who has to work.

SPECIALIST AND GARDENING HELP

A reliable electrician and plumber who will come at short notice are **essential**, unless you have the skills yourself. If not skilled at DIY, you will also need a jobbing builder who will turn up quickly in emergencies. As self-employed people, they will present a bill in the usual manner.

For doing defined jobs in the grounds, there should be no difficulty in finding someone to do it on a contract basis, or they may charge by the hour, but either way they are not directly employed by you. For employing a regular gardener either of the two cheque systems could be used. That is, if you can find someone. This is difficult because most men either have a regular job, or cannot cope with heavy work. You might, with luck, find a lady. As well as the usual gardening, they may need to look after the swimming pool, the bicycles, the stock of logs and any animals.

DOING BUSINESS WITH THE FRENCH

We found the French, on the whole, friendly and helpful. They are normally extremely polite. But I regret the world of business is rougher and tougher than the normal tourist encounters. French is a wonderful language for being rude. As a foreigner with a funny accent, you are an obvious target, though I doubt that it actually amounts to many more occasions than in the UK. Don't take it to heart. It'll be forgotten the next time you meet. You will get further and meet less resistance if you don't try to be too British all the time. Speak in French as much as possible, learn the correct forms of address, and don't put up notices in your establishment in English only.

The French can seem exasperatingly inefficient at times and you wonder how the *TGV* or *Concorde* ever got built. A letter arrives fixing an appointment for yesterday; someone arrives an hour late at a big meeting with no apology; Christmas decorations in a restaurant are still there in February. Just relax and accept that we northern Europeans and Americans perhaps value efficiency **for its own sake**; the southerners care about the end product, but **not** the means of getting there.

Among country people there is a great element of helping each other. Don't be afraid to ask for help and always accept it, if possible, when offered. Don't try to pay, or give any sort of 'thank you' gift. Just be prepared to help them out on some future occasion. The system works like savings in the bank; it's there when you need it and you will learn and gain a lot.

KEEPING UP THE STANDARD

Without any hotel experience, it's hard to know just what level of service is required. Well, it should be below a four-star hotel. The chocolate on the pillow at night, toilet paper folded to a V-shape, trouser press: all these belong to a more pretentious establishment. Yet you must not be too informal and homely. Bars of soap that have been used by someone else, cleaning materials left lying about, personal clothes left hanging in a cupboard: these won't do. Not all *chambres d'hôtes* undertake to 'service' (that means clean and make the beds) every day. If not, you would have to explain what to expect. Even if it's done on all other days, Sunday is particularly difficult. People are apt to stay around, so either you do the minimum or tell them 'not on Sundays' and they'll probably accept that. I've known hotels not accept new arrivals on Sundays but it would mean a loss of business.

It's hard to remember, but you **must** knock on bedroom doors and **wait** for an answer before entering, for obvious reasons. In your attire there's a difference between being casual and being sloppy. The universal jeans or shorts with T-shirt are fine for daytime, but you should change for dinner if you are serving. You will find that most of the guests change.

MANAGING YOUR TIME

If it all sounds like a great deal of hard work, well, it is in high season, therefore you must stop doing it all to impossible standards and wearing yourself out. Probably you came to France for the easy lifestyle, and here you are working 18-hour days. Examine everything to see if the work could be reduced, or the time spent carrying things about could be cut. Give yourself a proper break after lunch. Could the administration be reduced by more use of the computer? Could the cooking time be reduced, not by buying in products, but by timing the recipes and seeing which are quickest to prepare? Give yourself some privacy. With a couple of bedrooms there aren't too many people to worry about, but beyond that you could feel pressured. We had an objection to notices saying *privé* (private) at first. But, as the number of bedrooms climbed, we did put one on the kitchen door and on the door to our accommodation.

In the season the proprietor's day will look something like this if you do dinners (though not so neatly compartmentalised):

7–10am	Attending on guests and their breakfast, gardening
10–12.30	Housework, laundry, general maintenance
12.30–2.30pm	Relax
2.30–4pm	Some pre-prep for dinner, office work, ironing
4–5pm	Talking to guests and new arrivals
5–10pm	Preparing, serving, clearing guests' dinner
10–11pm	Tidying and locking up

If you have paid help, delegate. Let them get on with it. Give the cleaning person a list of the rooms to be cleaned *à fond* (thoroughly) for a changeover, and those to be tidied for people staying on. Then you must not be bothered any more. If there's no initiative to see what's needed, this isn't the right person. Don't ask her to come back next year. Tell the garden person the end result required and let them get on with it. Don't hover.

THE LONG WINTER MONTHS

As I said previously, in the early years and given that a B&B is seasonal you may want to find some paid employment for the winter month's. I'm afraid this will be very difficult unless you have a special skill to offer, and poor French language skills will not be tolerated. You can ask at the *mairie* about any organisations offering a home help service that you could join. This can be welcome paid employment.

THE PROPRIETORS

To give the true flavour of what it is like to run a *chambres d'hôtes*, I asked five proprietors to speak into a recording machine and tell me how it seems to them. It's noticeable how different they all are. In fact, one has now retired after ten years, three are in the thick of it, and one is just about to start. Here they are:

Anne

Anne and her husband bought their charming old mill house in 1989 and ran it as a *chambres d'hôtes* for ten years. They had six bedrooms, a one-bedroom *gîte* and a large garden with a swimming pool. They did not have a *table d'hôte*. Now they are retired.

After spending all our holidays in France we decided we liked the country so much we would retire there. However, we couldn't wait that long and, at 50, with our children gone to university, we decided to look for a suitable property to run as a *chambres d'hôtes* because we were too young to be completely retired. We found an old mill, very beautiful, habitable, but with possibility for renovation. So we arrived on my 50th birthday. There was an enormous amount of renovation, but we had our first guests, French, after three months.

Our mill was in a classified site so any exterior work had to be approved by the architect. My husband was very expert at building work. We had a French electrician and plumber, to help get things done quickly. It's good to employ French because we're living in their country. We did get a bit uptight when English or other nationalities come and bring their own materials for their workers from their own country.

Our guests were European, American, Russian, Australian. We got on very well with the French, and the locals accepted us and thought we were doing a good job. We opened the first winter, but there wasn't really any custom, and after two winters we decided only to open from Easter to October. The winters were spent decorating, building and preparing for the following year. If we did have a holiday, which was rare, that was at the end of the season in November. We went to Spain. When guests arrived we greeted them with smiles, even if it was raining, and a drink. Always smiling. Always smiling.

It was very expensive to employ anybody, so I had to do all the cleaning and the laundry, the changing of towels every day, the hanging on the line. My husband had to do all the grounds, the swimming pool, the general maintenance. That was onerous because we had too much land

and Englishmen like to keep their lawns mown. The bookings and administration were difficult during the season because you're also serving meals, drinks, smiling, and trying to answer the phone at the same time. We didn't have a great deal of trouble with the French tax, health insurance, etc., because we had registered and found the Chamber of Commerce very helpful.

We didn't belong to *Gîtes de France*. We were told we were too much like a hotel to be a *chambres d'hôtes*, and too much like a *chambres d'hôtes* to be a hotel. So I suppose we were a guest house. We advertised with *Chez Nous* and the *Sunday Times*. Word of mouth of course is very important.

We had high moments and low moments: trees falling down, electricity supplies cut. We had our own spring, and if the electricity was cut there was no water, but everybody seemed to understand. We had just lovely people. Lots of wonderful memories, but we reached 60 and decided that was enough. No regrets. Go for it; it's very rewarding if you're prepared to work hard.

Tony

Tony and his wife have run a *chambres d'hôtes* and *table d'hôte* for 13 years in a house in the centre of a medieval bastide town. There are six bedrooms, of which one is for the disabled on the ground floor, and a small garden for the guests' use. His wife had experience of hotel work before they came to France.

We'd always intended to open a small hotel or a *chambres d'hôtes*, but we plumped for a *chambres d'hôtes* as it is the ideal way of keeping a hands-on business. The *immoblier* advised that if we wanted an all-year-round business, it would not succeed in the country as we originally intended. We arrived before retirement age and had to make a living. Due to problems before we left, we arrived in France with only £2,000 in the bank. The result was we had to take out a mortgage. So we didn't exactly start off in a good way.

We had very little French then and I went to a few classes, but we learnt more by sitting at the dinner table with our French clients and a

French/English dictionary. We had quite a few entertaining evenings learning French. Answering the phone was a big problem, but after you've had the phone banged down several times because people couldn't understand, it focuses your mind wonderfully when you've got to earn a living. So we picked up French pretty quickly.

The property was in a good state when we bought it, but we had to put in six bathrooms. We had minimal problems with the building work, mainly because we did a lot of it ourselves. I think it's fair to say that you always have some problems with officialdom, but we'd run a small business in Britain and our experience is that problems are below the level with officials there.

We get on very well with the French, no problems that way at all. 60 per cent of our guests are French, 20 per cent English, and this year already we have had American and Australian, worldwide trade literally. In the 13 years we've been running the business, I can only think of less than ten times where we had a particular problem, and only twice have had to ask clients to leave. We do have problems with children. A *table d'hôte*, where everybody eats together is extremely reliant on the ambience. We do find the French and most of the other European children behave and are quite OK with the meals. But we find that Dutch and British children are an exception, in particular the British. This has caused a degree of embarrassment to us.

We have all-the-year-round business, though in winter it is probably 50 per cent of what we achieve in July and August. We always seem to have two or three bedrooms occupied. When there are no reservations we'll have a weekend in Spain or the Pyrenees. We very rarely visit the UK except when we have to: weddings, illnesses, funerals. The main reason is it's quite horrendous how expensive it is.

We don't mind getting up to do the breakfasts except when people say they particularly want breakfast at seven, roll down at eight, spend an hour having breakfast, and eventually we have to remind them that they should have left at eleven. We find that people do occasionally take advantage.

(This is Tony's wife speaking: The cooking isn't a problem. Our menus are French, but at first I wasn't au fait with the local cooking and a neighbour taught me. The only thing is that dinners happen at the end of the day and it is tiring.)

Now Tony again. I did find the housekeeping onerous at the beginning, but then I'd spent five years in the Air Force so it wasn't too difficult. I'm pleased we haven't got a swimming pool. We plan the garden for minimum maintenance. The bookkeeping we leave entirely to the accountant. We're not computer oriented at all.

We've never found French tax, health insurance, or social security difficult. But I think others could well have a different story. If we've got queries on tax, we go to the tax authorities direct, because they're the ones who decide. It doesn't matter if you've had an English adviser telling you that you don't do this or you don't do that. If the tax inspector at the local level says you pay it, you pay it. I think you pay an enormous amount for so called expert advice outside the system.

Advertising was difficult at the beginning because we were strapped for cash, so we first got into the *Guide de Routard*, and we soon found that we were getting into other guides, and now we're in 20, none of which do we pay for, unless we want a picture. So we spend about £600 a year.

I wouldn't have any hesitation in saying that it's an excellent way to earn a living if you want to come to France.

Anna

Anna and her husband bought an existing fully furnished *chambre d'hôte* business in 2005. It consists of a house and also a large barn converted into six bedrooms with a full height dining/billiard room and a kitchen. All the bedrooms open from the outside only onto a balcony or terrace and face the heated swimming pool. It is deep in the country and there is plenty of grounds and woodlands. There is also another small barn, at present derelict. They are just finishing their second season.

All the bedrooms have got en-suite shower rooms and work quite well but the mechanics of the swimming pool had been allowed to get into a terrible state of disrepair, so the electrics and heating and pumping had to be replaced. We do not have a separate *gîte* to let at the moment but we do let the whole *chambre d'hôte* building occasionally as a *gîte* for large parties. We do this for four to six weeks a year, as it gives us a little break from the routine. We've also got a ruin on site which is our long-term plan, once we get planning permission, to convert into our house and then the little house we're living in will be renovated to let.

We had access at the end of February and the first guests came at the beginning of April which presented us with a problem because there was a massive amount of work. We got it reasonably done in time. Building work hasn't been a problem because my husband is a builder, though locating equipment and the right materials and knowing whether you're paying the right price are difficult. We've not had a problem with officialdom yet, though I suspect we are about to have a massive one, but the *marie* is very well handled by a local farmer. The potential problem would appear to be that our business is at present classed as inactive.

We both enjoy meeting people and we have met the most incredible, interesting people. Though it's hard work dealing with people for a long period, even if they're wonderful, and sometimes it can be a bit of a strain. But it does provide a significant addition to our income. We get on very well with the French, bearing in mind that most of those we're dealing with we're usually spending money with, which influences things a little bit. Our neighbours are very easy going. We meet up with them but it's impossible to have the sort of relationship you would have with people speaking your own mother tongue. Perhaps you need to go to a class.

Most of our guests are English or English-speaking. We get the odd child; we don't actively encourage children because there's the awful problem with behaviour which seems to get worse. It's very difficult to allow people to come here for a peaceful retreat and then combine them with small monsters, especially English children.

All our advertising is done on UK main host sites. We do also find a lot of small sites where there's free advertising with a link to our own site which increases the exposure. We have concentrated on the development of our own web site which we can keep up to date; if your information is in endless different places you've got the problem of it being out of date. Most of our bookings come through the web.

In winter we close at the end of October. I think October is the most undersold month and I cannot understand why we could let the same room in August 20 times over. So next year we are pushing people into October with activity holidays and watercolour courses.

We do breakfast between nine and ten, as if it's later shopping and getting to the market in the morning is impossible. Evening meals are a constant bone of contention. People come here because it's possible to eat in, and they don't like going out, particularly once it's dark and they are terrified of the ditches. There aren't many places to eat close at hand, so I cook five or six nights a week in the season; we aren't rigid in saying which days, we play it by ear. Housekeeping is onerous. The laundry – I have never spent so much time discussing cleaning products as in the last two years, and how to get the towels white; I didn't even do that with nappies. All this towel washing is not environmentally friendly and it's expensive. I have a constant battle with fake tan, lipstick and other things. It makes me quite aggressive at times and I've sworn at some point to have black nylon sheets. I simply don't know what to do about it. We've tried to keep the rooms easy to clean, but there has to be a compromise between comfort and upkeep. We've added tea and coffee facilities to each room, except when there are small children. It creates a lot of work, but it's justified because a lot of people like tea in the morning.

The grounds need constant upkeep, as we try and have a lot of flowers. At the beginning of this year one of the best things we did was put in an irrigation system so that every new plant and tree on the site is watered automatically, which saves about two hours a day. The pool has a computerised system which copes with 16 people swimming one day and none the next, but they will cover themselves and children with oil and then swim. I understand, having had small children, but there has to be a better way than the amount of oil we get in the pool. We intend to have a solar heated shower next year.

I'm used to administration; the computer is on all the time and I see if there are any emails about a dozen times a day. We originally planned to see Europe but since we started this business we haven't got the time.

Philippe (who is French) and Brian (who is English)

This is the second chambre d'hôte they have run, the first house was too large, with big rooms impossible to heat economically. It was sold after a few years and, with the experience gained, they bought a more manageable house in 2006. Or rather, two small houses backing onto a courtyard in a medieval village, with a gigantic elaborately carved stone fireplace on the first floor and also the original stone spiral stair. Restoration was no problem to the architect partner who has designed the interior in a modern, almost minimalist, style with the aim of appealing to the very top end of the market. In fact they call it a maison d'hôte, they have a gourmet standard table d'hôte and examples of contemporary art are displayed throughout the house.

B: We bought this property because we wanted to be in the centre of the village. We have retained the original features that were here and then producing a contemporary environment for guests offering a high standard in our three guest bedrooms. It was in a fairly good state as a building but inside needing fourteen months of complete refurbishment and transformation. There was no heating system, no up to date electricity, no plumbing, the only toilet was in the courtyard and hadn't been used for about twenty five years. The roof had to be redone including the timber. The building work was quite expensive because the bedrooms had to have bathrooms ensuite and the soil pipes had to be chased into the existing walls. We have air conditioning and that had to be built into the structure. The fireplace was sort of collapsing and we had to reinforce the floor underneath. **P**: When you take on board such a project and are expecting to offer your guests the best standards you have to think about every possible detail and it would have been easier to rebuild the houses completely.

B: Unfortunately I do not speak French, I can manage one or two words; I had six months of classes but I am sorry to say I am not progressing as well as I should be. **P**: Fortunately I am French and I can deal with all the paperwork and administration, and using the French way of doing things the less you say to the official the better you are.

P: We start very early in the morning and finish very late at night, only five to six hour's sleep which is not very much. Our breakfasts are quite nice and setting up the table can take a good hour, so we have to spend two or three hours in all. **B**: We don't actually offer a cooked breakfast but if someone were to request a scrambled egg or salmon or things like that I would obviously do it. We offer home made confitures and muesli which I make.

P: Dinner is an extremely important part of the experience, we never get to bed before one, one-thirty because people spend a lot of time around the dining table. We spend a lot of time talking to them, also serving food, which we think is a high quality four course meal plated up as in a restaurant. **B**: We find that the issue of having to sit with our guests and talk and serve at the same time is too complex, as we are presenting our food at quite a high gourmet level. We have a vast selection of local and other French wines.

P: We are very hospitable and like people to think they are coming to a place which they can consider a home. Most of our guests staying with us here or in the past have become very good friends. The rooms are prepared with chocolates, mineral water and a complimentary bottle of wine. We have good quality linen changed daily. Obviously the housekeeping is a chore but then it's part of the service we offer. I spend a lot of time ironing the sheets; I had a machine but got rid of it because it didn't do it well enough. We have a housekeeper two or three times a week, and the courtyard we maintain ourselves. **B**: We don't encourage children but if someone wishes to bring a child we don't say no.

P: Unfortunately you can't run a business without an accountant and all that. **B**: At the moment we're not really advertising, it tends to be word of mouth and we do have a very good web site. We are now getting into one or two interesting magazines and articles are appearing about what we are doing here and this is bringing quite a response. We have very little holiday as we are open all year, perhaps short breaks. **P**: We're also going to other chambre d'hôtes to get an idea of the services our counterparts are offering to perhaps pick up on ideas that we can incorporate here. I would say that on top of everything else you have got to have one or two other activities to bring in enough money to live on because having a chambre d'hôte is an exciting experience and has got good sides, but even if you charge your clients a lot it's difficult.

P: I would say in conclusion that we want our guests to share something which is very different to bed and breakfast, we want them to share an art experience with us and with the wider project of our own exhibitions and displays in the house.

Maggie

Maggie and her husband bought their house in 2002 and are so new to the B&B business that they haven't yet received their first guest. Their house is in the country, but only a ten-minute drive to a town with one of the country's landmark historic abbeys. It is a farmhouse that had been renovated by the former owners to the highest standard I have ever seen, and with grounds and swimming pool to match. They will have a small *gîte* and three letting bedrooms all with an en-suite, but no other rooms specifically reserved for guests.

It's a beautiful house in a beautiful setting. We had considered doing the same thing in England, but the weather's not so good. We think we bought the right property because it's even better placed than we anticipated before moving in. The problem really is French; I am going to French classes twice a week. We decided to run a *chambres d'hôtes* because we've taken early retirement and we like meeting people.

It's not ideal for children; we'll probably accept children over ten but might have to change our ideas. It's definitely a bit windier than we thought and there's snow as well, but not consistently horrible like it is in the UK. We've been back to the UK once. I wondered if I would feel strange about coming back to France, but no, the joy of driving down an empty road and seeing the wonderful views made up for any qualms about leaving my sister and friends behind.

When we're up and running with the *chambres d'hôtes*, I would offer dinner by arrangement, probably three times a week, certainly on a Monday when things are closed, but I might change my mind and do more dinners. Breakfasts would be French style, I don't think there's any requirement to do the old English breakfast out here. The large garden was one of the reasons for buying the house, and, if the weather's hot, hopefully the plants won't grow too much. Probably one thing that would be tricky would be answering the phone initially, because I won't know if it's French people. If it is, then I have to struggle with the language a bit. We actually don't pay French tax at the moment, but we're going to sort it out because it would be beneficial for us to pay French tax rather than English. We've already sorted out our social security and we're awaiting our *Cartes de Séjour*. Amazingly, you're told that French bureaucracy is difficult; we just walked in and walked out; much easier than doing anything in the UK really.

We haven't decided where to advertise yet, but we're hoping to pick up bookings through the internet. My daughter-in-law is going to do us a web site. I'm going to have some printed literature done and take it to estate agents, and then we'll register with *Gîtes de France* because that's the only way the tourist office will accept us. One or two people have given me ideas of companies to advertise with that won't cost too much, because we're a small concern and haven't got that many rooms to let out. I really hope it works out because I'm getting quite excited about it all now. It's a big learning curve and any assistance from people locally on what to do and how to go about it is always welcomed. Hopefully, this time next year we'll be able to say, 'Oh look, we've got several people booked already, and repeats from last year'. So I wish us luck, even though I shouldn't say it myself.

TIPS FOR MAKING IT PAY

◆ Be there when guests arrive, personally take them to their room, and offer a welcoming drink.

◆ Take up references on anyone you employ; a mistake could be costly.

◆ Don't wear yourself out by doing it all yourself.

TIP FOR IMPROVING YOUR FRENCH

◆ Always reply in French to French people, even when they try to help you out in English.

14

Keeping the Customers Happy

Who are they, these people who come as strangers and leave as friends?

NATIONALITY

This depends partly on your location and partly on where you advertise. If situated near the channel ports, you will receive mostly British people. In fact some of these B&Bs find their clientele is almost exclusively British through no particular desire on their part, just a result of proximity to the ports. Others set out deliberately to have only British guests and I personally think this is a mistake. The French guests that do arrive will not like being entirely surrounded by the English language, and I think the British guests are losing out too, because surely they haven't come to France just to meet their own kind. I strongly recommend you to give a warm welcome to all the world; it's much more interesting for all concerned. Anyway, one tends to have preconceived notions about nationality before people arrive. So many are on the move these days: we had British living in Spain, France, Czechoslovakia; Australians in Hong Kong, France, UK; the world's a real *pot-pourri* these days. Yet they were all taking a holiday in France.

We achieved:	Another British B&B:	National Average:
40% French	60% French	75% French
30% British	20% British	25% Rest
10% Benelux	20% Rest	
20% Rest		

You will see we did our very best to make the French welcome, but still got the backhanded compliment in our visitors' book from a military gentleman that we were 'a little bit of England in a French zone'. Owners will always have proportionally more of their own nationality because, of course, that's where they advertise.

The up-and-coming countries are believed to be in eastern Europe. We were taken aback one day when an expensive sports car drew up and the owner explained he was from Lithuania 'next to Russia'. Regretfully, he doesn't feature in our visitors' book as we were full. Have you any ideas for being ahead of the pack and cultivating their custom?

AGE

Staying in a *chambres d'hôtes* is very much the holiday choice for the 45 to 65 age group, so a lot of the customers are near retiring, early retired or already retired and you must bear this in mind when setting up your establishment. The next group is couples with babies and young children. There will be hardly any teenagers unless they happen to be en route to somewhere else. Young adults will only come if there is a sporting facility. Then there are a few quite frail elderly people; our oldest was 95.

HOLIDAYS

You will be disappointed to find that people **do not** come and stay for nice neat periods for a fortnight's holiday, Saturday to Saturday. Certainly, the majority of guests will be on holiday, but this has many variations. If you are in the country, or near the sea or mountains, then you will get the long-stay holiday customers, though people are restless these days and not many stay for a fortnight; a week is more usual. Just very exceptionally, there are those who stay three weeks, especially, with children. Far more common is a two- to four-night stay, and these are the people most likely to come back again and again. But for 75 per cent of B&Bs, the **mainstay of the business is one-night guests**.

FRENCH NAME	ENGLISH NAME	DATE	COMMENTS
Jour de l'An	New Year's Day	1st Jan	Public holiday
Jour des Rois	Twelfth Night	6th Jan	—
Mardi-Gras	Shrove Tuesday	Feb/Mar	—
Le 1 Avril	All Fools' Day	1st April	—
Vendredi Saint	Good Friday	Mar/Apr	Not a holiday
Pâques	Easter	Mar/Apr	Sunday
Pâques	Easter Monday	Mar/Apr	Public holiday
Fête du Travail	May Bank Holiday	1st May	Public holiday
Victoire 1945	VE Day	8th May	Public holiday
Ascension	Ascension Day	Varies	Public holiday
Pentecôte	Whitsun	Varies	Public holiday on Monday after
Fête Nationale	—	14th July	Public holiday
Assomption	Feast of the Assumption	15th August	Public holiday
Rentrée	Start of School Year	1st week in September	—
Halloween	Halloween	31st October	—
Toussaint	All Saint's Day	1st November	Public holiday
Armistice 1918	Remembrance Day	11th November	Public holiday
—	Christmas Eve	—	Not celebrated
Noël	Christmas Day	25th December	Public Holiday
—	Boxing Day	—	Not celebrated
Fête Ste Sylvestre	New Year's Eve	31st December	—

Figure 35 The French Year

OTHER REASONS FOR COMING

You will be amazed at all the other reasons why people are staying with you. The two most frequent with us were house hunting and attending a wedding. But there were many others: first communion, house warming, golden wedding, visiting sick relative, funeral, and of course many people didn't say. The house hunting group would be better described as 'property generally' because it also encompassed: selling, moving in or out, or keeping an eye on the building work. To give an idea of numbers, we can name 22 couples who stayed with us in connection with a property they own locally, and a great many more who were 'just looking'. It's a great source of out-of-season business.

People attending weddings were concentrated in the high season, especially the Saturdays nearest the 14th July and 15th August holidays. We had three or four groups a year, mostly French, but some British. Getting married in the country is quite the thing for the French, and for Brits too it's fashionable to marry in France, if there are parents living there to do the honours. The tourist office often provided the names of all the local hostelries for the wedding organiser to send out to the guests for them to make their choice. However some B&Bs are not thrilled by wedding guests in high season as they seldom have dinner, and most only stay for the Saturday night.

You may be hoping to fill the rooms out of season with business people. In a town this will happen, and they can go out in the evenings. But in the country there will be hardly any, and they usually prefer a hotel with a bar. You may be lucky enough to find the occasional person working locally who needs temporary lodgings in the winter, perhaps for a week, perhaps three months. But they will want a **very** reduced price, out of which you have got to provide heating, and would need to discuss carefully what meals they want.

WHEN DO THEY COME?

These days a fortnight's stay in one place is rare, especially in a B&B, but most people now take several holidays a year. One of the prime reasons for having an international clientele is to try and lengthen the season; however, out-of-season stays are mostly only a couple of days.

The French are totally wedded to the six weeks comprising the second half of July and August. There is an old chestnut of a story in which a couple pretended to be away in August by shutting themselves in for the month, when actually they couldn't afford to go away. A Frenchman said to us,

'Now I am retired I can take my holiday early'. He meant the first week of July. Even for the French the last week of August is not so popular for couples with children because there is a long list of equipment for school that has to be purchased, and the list is not issued earlier. You will receive some custom for weekends and half terms and this is a very good reason for encouraging a French clientele.

The Scandinavians, Dutch and Belgians start their school summer holiday earlier than France or Britain, so they are likely to come at the beginning of July.

Unfortunately, many British couples without children still go away in the school holidays, either because they work in education, or they used to and don't want to change, or they like to holiday at the same time as grandchildren. The British and American 'slightly older' couples favour September.

Until recently, foreigners only came for weekends and half-terms to areas near their own country. Now the introduction of cheap flights to provincial airports has made short-stay and out-of-season trips feasible much further afield. But short breaks are still only popular for the mid-season periods; it's all but impossible to do much in the winter, except for skiing.

THE WELCOME (*L'Accueil*)

The French set great store by the welcome they receive on arrival. It is mentioned over and over again in the literature on *chambres d'hôtes*. This puzzled me for a long time, because **of course** the guests will be made welcome with a big smile, a handshake, being shown personally to their room, and then sat down with a cup of tea or coffee. What else? A proprietor is in business to make a living, if the guests don't like the welcome they might leave and certainly won't come again. I asked a French friend for an explanation and was told that in a hotel you are given a key by a po faced receptionist and told to find the room yourself, at least anywhere less than five stars. The fact is, it is in the French nature to be cautious and it's revealing that their word *étranger* means 'outsider' or 'stranger' as well as 'foreigner'. They feel you cannot know if an *étranger* is to be trusted, so it's better to keep your distance. To smile straight away is superficial, much later on it will mean something.

Therefore a *chambres d'hôtes* proprietor has got to be un-French to a remarkable degree. To us and the Americans it's second nature to smile and be pleasant. We are taught that from an early age, so we can't see the problem. Nevertheless, do be a bit careful with the welcome, it is just possible they have come for a funeral. In fact be guided by the customer as to how friendly and chatty they want to be. Don't be intrusive but let people know where to find you if they need any help.

ETIQUETTE

This is always a problem in another country. As a visitor you will be forgiven much, but in business you are expected to know. In France you **must** use the local manners. When opening the front door to a stranger it is up to you to speak first. If you don't know what language say 'bonjour, hello' and let them respond. When it's guests arriving, the first thing is to shake hands with everyone, and I mean **everyone**, it is impolite to leave anyone out, even children, though for children under five you could ask their name by way of a greeting. Say *bonjour* to everyone the first time you meet them every day. But it is not polite to say it again because that means you have forgotten the earlier meeting.

During the day at least one of the patrons should try and say some pleasantry to each guest. First names are not used nearly as much as we do; you would need to know the guest well, but modify this according to age of guest. In fact, on the first greeting, you should not even use the surname, it's *bonjour, madame/monsieur*. After about 6pm it's *bonsoir* and this means 'hello' as well as 'goodbye'. After a couple of days you could add to your *bonjour* the words *ça va?* which means literally 'how goes it?'. The other will probably reply *ça va*. It's just like the English 'how do you do', where the reply is not expected to be full details of your latest operation.

A particular difficulty for Anglophones is the use of the second person singular which has totally disappeared from our everyday language. It **must** be used to children under about ten, to animals, and when speaking to your spouse. Since it needs a completely different set of verb endings it needs some nimble thinking. Use the word *madame* to all women over about 18; it doesn't have the connotation of being married any more than the English use of Mr to all males.

When people leave, you do the hand-shaking routine all over again, but this time a young child may raise it's head for a kiss, in which case go ahead. Otherwise you do not kiss the paying guests. From the B&B viewpoint, the French are so good at departures. They load up the car and the **very last thing** is for them all to come and say goodbye. Then you know they've gone and you can go and do their room. The British are so wishy-washy, they can drift about for half an hour saying goodbye, or sometimes they don't bother. If you've got to shake everyone's hand, then they will expect to reciprocate, and all the patrons should try and be present at departures, though it's not always possible. Then when we waved them off as they went down the drive it was like continually saying goodbye to friends; actually it's a bit wearing by the end of the season because it could add up to 500 people.

When foreigners choose to stay in a *chambres d'hôtes* in France, they will expect to encounter the French way of life, so it's not necessary to modify your approach to each, though sometimes they will look puzzled by your outstretched hand.

In everyday speech and on the phone, your French will sound very stilted because you lack all the little interjections. Try some of the following:

oui=bien sûr (certainly)	*non=je regrette* (I'm sorry)
d'accord (agreed)	*désolé* (extremely sorry)
pas de problème (no problem)	*impossible* (impossible)
ah bon (oh good)	
tout à fait (quite so)	
pas de tout (not at all)	
avec plaisir (with pleasure)	
parfait (splendid, perfect)	

CHILDREN

The possibilities are:

1. Be as child-friendly as possible.

2. Do nothing special and you won't get many.

3. Don't allow children at all: difficult if you accept one night stays.

In fact, you don't get that many British children as it's not a holiday type that has ever been marketed specially for them. This is fortunate perhaps, as they are so badly behaved, or am I being too censorious of my compatriots? The children we had were mostly French and Belgian and on a wet day they were sat down at the dining-table by their parents to do extra homework without evident complaint. We noticed that parents often expected to find other children for theirs to play with, but it was most unlikely for there to be any of the same age.

Children are a great responsibility, and you must do your best with safety precautions so that you won't be criticised if there is an accident. Also, of course you're expected to have a very reduced price for children, and even be totally free for babies. Children need a lot of equipment to keep them amused, they break things, they lose things, they're noisy, they are a nuisance at table, and they wet the bed. But in spite of all those things, they're a joy to have around and we did as much as possible to encourage families.

Babies

You need a cot and high-chair even though many parents bring their own. We expected parents to bring their own baby food which we would heat in our microwave. This is where a kitchenette for the guests is most convenient, otherwise parents are likely to invade your kitchen at any time of the day. We only had two or three babies a year, and there were never any complaints about them crying, or were the other guests being polite?

Toddlers

They are much more of a problem and their safety is a worry. We didn't have a gate at the top of the stairs as I couldn't see other guests remembering to shut it. Maybe we should have. Ornaments need lifting above child head height. Parents generally bring plenty of toys, so don't provide much, and certainly not books which won't last five minutes. On no account take on baby sitting or child-minding. Explain that you are not insured for this.

Five to twelve years

Older children need occupying and this is where most of your equipment should be directed. They will monopolise the pool of course, and will be prime users of everything else. They will also poke into places where they shouldn't, so all stores should be locked. They need amusing indoors too – the TV of course, also board games, cards, table-football, table tennis, whatever you can provide. Unless you are actively watching children in some activity, **do not** let the parents expect you to keep an eye on them while you are working. A horror story I heard was that the parents went for a walk, leaving the children to play in the garden. Well, those children cut off the cat's whiskers and rode on the dog such that its back was injured and it had to be put down.

Teenagers

French teenagers holiday with their parents longer than other nationalities, but it is quite beyond your scope to provide for them. Just direct them to your brochure display stand where they will find info. on riding stables, quad cars, championship size swimming pool, tennis courts, etc. They eat a lot too, except girls who are slimming.

DISABLED AND ELDERLY CUSTOMERS

Some of our customers were very frail looking, and that was a worry too. Well, it's their choice if they're still travelling, but when I saw them trying to park, I did wish they weren't still driving. Elderly people usually have small appetites and would appreciate a reduced meal.

A bathroom for the disabled does look a bit institutional, but the facilities are also appreciated by couples with a baby. And bear in mind that some people are temporarily disabled, for example by having a leg in plaster.

Naturally you should not refuse to take the very occasional mentally handicapped person. Your attitude will influence the other guests' reaction. Remove small objects from the room, and if meals look like being a problem suggest a different time.

CUSTOMERS' ANIMALS

Mainland Europeans have always liked to bring their dogs and cats on holiday. I am sure that Brits will too, more and more now that it is possible. Do you want them? We stated that we did not accept animals, but occasionally could be persuaded. At least then we could refuse if we wanted to. Although people don't like extras, I would make a charge for animals so that you've got some recompense for the one in ten that will do some damage. If you don't take animals, what will you do about the people who forgot to mention they had one? Just sigh, accept them, and charge.

On all that land in the country could you stable horses and, if near a hiking trail, donkeys too? Either in stables or in a field with an electric fence, there's quite a call for it. Or perhaps come to an arrangement with a near neighbour.

CUSTOMERS YOU COULD DO WITHOUT

Fortunately few, but you will get one or two. Prize bores at the table were one of the lesser hazards. For complaints the golden rule is to respond immediately. Unfortunately the aggro usually flares up when more than one thing has gone wrong. Sometimes it is your fault, sometimes theirs, but it all adds up to an unpleasant explosion. Hold you temper; don't make excuses – they only sound lame. Then do your utmost to put right whatever is wrong **immediately**, though sometimes this is impossible. The plumber or electrician won't come in under 24 hours; the spare part needs ordering. Only offer a refund as a last resort; better to offer a good bottle of wine. Keep the discussion away from other guests or it will upset them too. Don't take it to heart; it happens to all proprietors sooner or later.

TOURIST INFORMATION

Guests will very much appreciate a folder in their room containing your own and other tourist information. It looks like a lot of work but in fact is a good promotion tool which it's a shame to miss. People can be seen sitting outdoors diligently reading it. It can consist of loose leaves in a hard cover ring binder; have it in French on one page and in English on the facing page; put your name and logo on each page and include a photo on as many pages as possible. I'm assuming you'll do this on a computer, and if you're not adept at desk top publishing you soon will be. It's really for the long stay visitor, because for one or two rooms it's not worth it. Have a page for most of the following:

'Welcome'
Prices and special offers
House procedures for keys, room cleaning and changing linen, clothes washing, swimming pool, early breakfast, paying, items left behind
Local attractions including those specially for children
Local sports facilities: tennis, golf, fishing, riding, swimming, and any others available
Dinners: price, reservation, hour, special diets, sample menu
Scan in visiting cards of local restaurants and note distances and closing days
Local *commerces*: bank, market, supermarket, chemist, post office, hairdresser, etc.
Travel: garages, car hire, bicycle hire, taxis, buses (if any), station
Church services
Nearest doctor, dentist and chiropodist
Local walks if the Tourist Office has made up the info
Whole and half-day excursions by car with a red line drawn on a map
Selection of nice comments from the visitors' book (don't be modest)

You are expected to be a fount of local knowledge. It's all part of the service to advise the clients on their itineraries, shopping, restaurants, sports facilities and where to buy organic walnut oil. If you don't have a visitors' folder as prescribed above, buy a set of display stands for all your literature or it will need tidying every day. And even with a folder it's a good idea to have a large pin-up board for forthcoming events. One event everyone is interested in is the *meteo* (weather forecast); a 24-hour forecast is obtainable on www.meteo.fr/meteonet/temps/france/prev/frprev.htm, but there is a charge for a four- or seven-day forecast.

The emergency number is **not** 999, so a list should be attached to the telephone:

SAMU (ambulance)	15
Police	17
Pompiers (fire)	18
English speaking emergency	112 (all services)

STRANGERS IN A FOREIGN LAND

Sometimes the help guests ask for goes well beyond the standard queries. Be a little cautious; it can take up a lot of time, and if it's medical, you may not be the right person to help. By all means give local lifts as a good will gesture, but do not ferry people to airports, stations, etc. You are not insured to take passengers and you don't know how much to charge. If they are in a fix, they'll just have to take a taxi.

Very few of your guests will have absolutely no French or English. I can only remember three jolly Italian taxi drivers (visiting France for a dog show, of course), and an Argentinian family. But this is not to say they can all converse fluently and they too will have difficulties on the phone. They may ask you to make a reservation at a restaurant, or book their next night's stay. Take this on just to be helpful. For most guests, language didn't seem to matter as long as people were friendly. We felt it was only the Brits who worried about a 'language problem'.

THE FINAL ANALYSIS

Guests like

Good instructions and signposts for finding you
A friendly welcome
Oak beams

Log fires
Meals out of doors
Central heating
Everything super clean
Toile de Jouy fabrics and wallpapers
Fluffy towels
Plenty of pillows
Home produce
Home cooking
Enough sun loungers
You as the host remembering their name

Guests do not like

Hosts not living in the same building
Tiny rooms
Anything broken or not working
Less than standard-size beds
A fixed breakfast time
Stale bread
A meagre breakfast
Noisy plumbing, traffic or televisions
Rodents, insects or reptiles indoors
Cold bathrooms
Cramped showers
Intrusive household pets
Pinned up notices
No dessert
Everything closed up at 9pm

THE END OF THE DAY

Until my children were well into their teens, I used to look in on them before going to bed, just to check they were all right. Obviously I didn't look into the guests' bedrooms, but as I went round the house a little before midnight, locking the outside doors, closing windows and turning off lights, it did seem as if I was checking that all was well with the people in my charge again.

TIPS FOR MAKING IT PAY

◆ Aim for a worldwide clientele to lengthen the season.

◆ Deal with complaints promptly and give a free bottle of wine, not a discount.

TIP FOR IMPROVING YOUR FRENCH

◆ *Lisez un roman en français.*

Postscript

Having read this far I assume you are seriously contemplating a life across the Channel and it seems appropriate to include a final few words of encouragement about France and the French.

Firstly it is, like Britain, a settled, cultured land with all the services you would expect, where freedom of speech, movement and published opinion are guaranteed under the law. In short it is a modern democratic society.

As for the French themselves, there is a persistent myth that they are unfriendly, difficult and somehow unacceptably idiosyncratic. All nations have characteristics peculiar to their society, including the British of course. '*Vive la différence*', as the French themselves would say. Don't waste time making unfavourable comparisons, as if Britain was a repository of all the virtues. It isn't, and we can learn something from the French, for example their concern for family values and quality of life.

Personal difficulties spring mostly from misunderstandings or misconceptions. If offence is caused either way, and it will happen sometimes, well that's life. It could happen anywhere in the world.

Our own experience has been overwhelmingly positive. We have been accepted with genuine warmth and friendliness and have no regrets in adapting to the French way of life.

By meeting the French half way and making yourself aware of their social code without prejudice or preconceptions, you are embarking on an enriching experience.

Le dernier qui quittera l'Angleterre est prié d'éteindre la lumière

200

Appendix A – Useful Books

All titles are in English except where stated. Cookbooks are too numerous to mention, so take your pick from any bookshop: only a few books of special interest are included here. If you are already living in France note that www.amazon.fr stocks most of the books in English that the UK site has and the postage is less.

Understanding the French

France In The New Century/John Ardagh/Penguin Books/2000
  'Portrait of a changing society'.
French Or Foe?/Polly Platt/Culture Crossings/1994
  An American looks at life and business in France.
Sixty Million Frenchmen Can't Be Wrong/Jean-Benôit Nadeau & Julie Barlow/Robson Books/2004
  A serious study of what makes the French so French.

Advice for newcomers

France: A Handbook For New Residents/M. Michael Brady/Howtobooks/2007
  Set out in encyclopaedia style for easy reference.
Live & Work in France/Victoria Pybus/Vacation-Work/2005
  Tells you the basics, including what to do when things go wrong.
Living & Working In France/David Hampshire/Survival Books/2006
  More useful to recent arrivals still baffled by the complexities.
Pardon My French/Charles Timmoney/Penguin Books/2007
  One of the best self-help manuals.

Language

Cassell's French Dictionary/Cassell Modern Language Dictionaries/1997
  At over £90 this is the most expensive book you'll ever buy. Worth it if you're serious about learning French.

French Verb Tables/Collins Gem/2001
  Essential.
Visual French Dictionary/Jean-Claude Corbeil & Ariane Archambault/
  Oxford University Press/2003
  All entries are illustrated in colour.

Buying

Buying A Home In France/David Hampshire/Survival Books/2006
  Good, but one of many.
Buying A Home In France/Peter Macbride & Monique Perceau/Hodder
  Headline/2005
  A good basic guide with the emphasis on vocabulary, including building
  materials.
Buying A Property In France/Clive Kristan/Howtobooks/2003
  Good, but one of many.
Buying & Renovating A Property In France/Richard Whiting/Howtobooks/
  2007
  Good, but one of many.
The Complete Guide To Buying Property In France/Charles Davey/Kogan
  Page/2004
  For the complete newcomer.
Les Plus Beaux Villages de France/Maurice Chalbert/Readers Digest/2005
  In French, so choose your village from the complete list.

Renovating

Dictionary Of French Building Terms/Richard Wiles/Summersdale
  Publishers/2006
  Comprehensive enough for all DIY work.
How To Renovate A House In France/Ackers, Aumont & Carslake/Accent
  Publishing/2004
  They build differently in France.
Renovating & Maintaining Your French Home/Joe Laredo/Survival
  Books/2007
  Plenty of advice.
Vivons Perchés/Alain Laurens/Edition de la Martinière
  In French, itemising 50 original tree houses.

Interiors

The French Room/Elizabeth Wilhide/Conran Octopus/1995
  'Simple French style for your home'.

Exteriors

Mediterranean Gardening/Hilda Gildermeister/University of California
  Press/2002
  'A waterwise approach'. Gardening in a different climate is not easy.
Natural Swimming Pools/Michael Littlewood/Schiffer Design Book/2005
  'Inspiration for harmony with nature'.
Pool Idea Book/Lee Anne White/Taunton Home Idea Book/2006
  Instead of the standard rectangle have a pool designed by a professional.
Poolscaping/Catriona Tudor Erler/Storey Books US/2003
  'Gardening & landscaping around your pool & spa'.
The Ultimate Guide To Pool Maintenance/Terry Taminen/Mcgraw-Hill
  Professional/2007
  There's no escape, a pool has got to be well maintained.

Officialdom

Starting A Business In France/Richard Whiting/Howtobooks/2006
  There's a better chance of success if you've done the research.
Taxation In France 2003/Charles Parkinson/PKF/2003
  Clearly presented for those who want to know about taxation in detail.

Food

The Cooktionary/Gee Greville/Franglivres/2003
  A French dictionary for cooks. Self-published, but can be obtained from
  'French News' – see under Useful Addresses.
Crumbles/Camille le Foll/Marabout Coté Cuisine/2002
  Crumble is a trendy dessert in France and this book is written in French.
Well Preserved/Joan Hassol/Prentice Hall & IBD/1998
  'A jam making hymnal'.

Household

How Clean Is Your House?/Kim Woodburn & Aggie Mackenzie/Michael
  Joseph/2004
  Your guests will be quick to notice any failings.

Mrs Beeton's Book of Household Management/Isabella Beeton/Facsimile
Edition/Chancellor Press
For the household management, not the recipes.
The Penny Pincher's Book Revisited/John & Irma Mustoe/Souvenir
Press/2007
Some of these ideas are worth using in a B&B, if they don't take up any
extra time.

Appendix B – Useful Addresses

Always drop the first '0' when telephoning from another country. Numbers beginning with '08' cannot be dialled from another country.

British Officialdom

British Embassy, 35 rue de Faubourg St Honoré, 75008 Paris, France.
  Tel: 01 44 51 31 02

Department of Social Security, Overseas Benefits Directorate (Med), Longbenton, Newcastle on Tyne NE98 1YX.
  (For National Health)

Inland Revenue National Insurance Contributions Office, Longbenton, Newcastle on Tyne NE98 1ZZ.
  Tel: 0191 225 5811
  (For pensions)

Cookery course

Leiths School of Food & Wine, 21 St Albans Grove, London W1 5BP.
  Tel: 020 7229 0177
  Web: www.leiths.com

Language courses

Alliance Française, 1 Dorset Square, London NW1 6PU.
  Tel: 020 7224 1865
  Web: www.alliancefrancaise.org.uk

BBC
  WEb: www.bbc.co.uk/languages/french

Berlitz
  Web: www.berlitz.co.uk

Hotcourses
  (Directory of full time, part time, evening, weekend, courses; searchable
    by region and city)
  Web: www.hotcourses.com
Institut Francais, Language Centre, 14 Cromwell Place, London SW7 2JR.
  Tel: 020 7581 2707
  Web: www.institut-francais.org.uk
Open University, Walton Hall, Milton Keynes MK7 6AA.
  Tel: 01908 659141
  www/open.ac.uk

Magazines and newspapers
Accueillir Magazine, 332 rue Lecourbe, 75015 Paris
  For chambre d'hôtes proprietors, in French)
  Web: www.accueillir-magazine.com
France, Digbeth Street, Stow On The Wold, Glos. GL54 1BN.
  (For background information)
  Tel: 01451 831398
  Web: www.francemag.com
French Property News, 6 Burgess Mews, London SW19 1UF.
  (For property exhibitions and property for sale)
  Tel: 020 8543 3113
  Web: www.french-property-news.com
The Lady, 39–40 Bedford Street, London WC2E 9ER.
  Tel: 01451 831398
  Web: www.thelady.co.uk
The News, 5 Chemin de la Monzie, BP 4042, 24004 Périgueux, France.
  (Gives help and information to new residents)
  Tel: 05 53 06 84 40
The Oldie, 65 Newman Street, London W1T 3EG.
  Tel: 020 7565 3188
  Web: www.theoldie.co.uk

Mail order

General catalogues

La Redoute, 59081 Roubaix Cedex 2, France.

Tel: 08 92 350 350

Web: www.laredoute.fr

3 Suisses, 59345 Croix Cedex.

Tel: 08 92 69 15 00

Web: www.3suisses.fr

Hotel Linen

Linvosges Hôtellerie, 6 place de la Gare, 88400 Gerardmer, France.

Tel: 08 92 68 88 03

Web: www.linvosges.com

Miscellaneous

Chèques-Vacances, 5 rue Gabriel Pri, 92584 Clichy Cedex, France.

Tel: 0891 670 570

Web: www.ancv.com

French Chamber of Commerce, 21 Dartmouth St, London SW1H 9HP.

(Get their book *Setting Up A Business In France*)

Tel: 020 7304 4040

French Government Tourist Office, 178 Piccadilly, London W1V OAL.

Tel: 0171 491 7622

Maisons Paysannes de France, 8 passage des deux Sœurs, 75009 Paris

Tel: 01 44 83 63 63

Web: www.maisons-paysannes.org

Piscines Waterair, ZA, 68580 Seppois-le-Bas, France.

(Steel lined swimming pools)

Tel: (in France) 0 825 00 05 58

Web: www.waterair.com

Index

Accueil Paysan, 17, 151
accountant, 111, 115
activity holidays, 143
administration, 102
advertising, 16, 143, 148, 154
age, 186
agriculture, 78
airing cupboard, 45, 122
ambiance, 45, 50
ambulance, 137
animals, 78, 160, 161, 172, 195
answerphone, 111
architect, 23, 26, 36, 37
arm chairs, 54, 64, 65, 71
art classes, 144, 145
asbestos, 25
attic, 68

babies, 186
badminton, 79, 114
bank account, 28, 129, 130
barbeque, 73, 91, 92, 97, 142
barns, 28, 35, 45, 70, 71, 72
basin, 58
bath, 57
bathroom, 5, 6, 31, 32, 34, 35, 43, 46,
    55, 57, 117, 161
B&B guides, 154, 155, 156, 157, 158
bedrooms, 5, 6, 7, 9, 14, 21, 32, 34, 53,
    54, 55, 68, 92, 100, 106, 148, 160, 161
beds, 53, 54, 117
bedspreads, 56, 113, 116, 118
beverage, 83, 84, 135

bicycles, 72, 79, 114, 172
bidet, 59
bills, 111, 115, 171
billiards, 66
bis roads, 17
black, 138
blankets, 115, 116, 120
bolsters, 3, 115
booking, 88, 107, 148, 153
book-keeping, 115
bottle bank, 81
boules, 79
bread, 83, 84, 93
bread oven, 33, 34
breakfast, 32, 61, 83, 85, 106, 135, 150
breakfast cereal, 85
brick, 42
British Embassy, 138
brochure, 16, 83, 88, 92, 154, 163, 165
builders, 26, 37, 38
building regulations, 36
bunks, 54
business name, 164
business rates, 131
butter, 79, 85, 92
buying, 23

cake, 84
camping, 171
cancellations, 110
car, 115, 168
carpet, 43, 52, 60, 62
cases, 54

Centre des Impôts, 131
Certificat d'Urbanisme, 27, 28, 35
Chambre d'Agriculture, 78, 80
Chambre de Commerce, 128
cheese, 83, 92, 93
chef, 88, 97, 100
chemist, 134
Chéque Emploi Service, 169
Chéques Vacances, 165
chest of drawers, 54
children, 16, 47, 54, 77, 89, 161, 169,
  170, 188, 193
chimney, 42
chimney fire, 115
chlorine, 75
Christmas, 98, 107
classes, 4, 143
cleaning, 7, 66, 67, 77, 113, 117, 142
cleaning lady, 169
clés, 152
Clévacances, 150, 152
coffee, 94
cold meats, 83
company, 27, 129
complaints, 194
completion, 27, 28, 29
computer, 68, 111, 112, 173
conditional clause, 26
conservatory, 32
cot, 54, 192
credit card, 110, 130
crockery, 90
croissant, 16, 84
curtains, 118, 121
customers, 17, 185
cutlery, 90, 96

damp proof course, 42
dates, 110
deeds, 29

demi-pension, 89, 96, 97
demolition, 36
dentist, 168, 195
deposit, 109
desk, 68
dessert, 94
diets, 96
dining room, 33, 62
dinner, 17, 18, 61, 64, 67, 87, 88, 97, 98,
  99, 142, 161, 169
directories, 158
disabled, 34, 48, 60, 194
dishwasher, 46, 61, 96
DIY, 41, 60, 169, 171
doctor, 134, 195
doors, 35, 44
double booking, 107
drainage, 36, 47
dressing table, 54
drinks, 95
dryer, 68, 122
duvet, 118, 120

eggs, 84
elderly customers, 80, 194
electrician, 46, 171
electricity, 22, 25, 29, 46, 56, 115, 137,
  138
e-mail, 112, 153, 168
entree, 92
épis, 4, 20, 21 35, 104, 150, 152
estate agent, 23, 24
etiquette, 190
euro, 29, 104, 106
exchange rate, 29, 134
extension:
  building, 32, 34, 36
  telephone, 112

facture, 111

failure, 9
farm, 17, 141
farming, 135, 140, 141
ferme auberge, 15, 144, 149
finance, 103
fire, 45
fire extinguisher, 62, 66
fireplace, 149
fire service, 137
fixtures and fittings, 28
Fleurs de Soleil, 151
floors, 43, 55, 61, 64, 144
flowers, 56, 66, 78, 126, 159
freebies, 126
frozen food, 99
fruit, 83, 159

games room, 66
garage, 35
garden, 72
gardener, 172
gas, 29, 45, 47, 61, 115, 138
gazumping, 24
general contractor, 37, 72
gîtes, 3, 4, 7, 15, 33, 142, 146, 161
Gîtes de France, 3, 66, 72, 89, 91, 109,
  141, 149, 152
glasses, 90
golf, 79
goodwill, 14
gourmet, 34, 97
Grandes Randonnées, 19
grants, 103
guest house, 3
guides, 118, 154, 155, 158
gutters, 42

hall, 66
health care, 132
heating, 5, 45, 56, 64, 144, 189

hedges, 80
herb tea, 84, 100
holidays, 20, 168, 170, 187, 189, 190
honey, 85
hosts, 89
housing estates, 149

identity card, 129
income tax, 128, 131
insulation, 43, 45
insurance, 113, 144
ironing machine, 117

jam, 79, 85

keys, 53
kitchen, 33, 61, 67, 123, 144

land, 21, 22
Land Registry, 28
land surveyor, 23, 28
laundry, 122, 137, 142, 144
library, 64
licence:
  drinks, 135
  driving, 136
  TV, 136
lieu-dit, 164
linen, 118, 142
linen cupboard, 67
livret de famille, 130
location, 15, 22
logo, 149, 160, 165
logs, 80
loss, 5
lounge, 64
lunch, 38, 86, 90, 161, 173

magazines, 137, 150 158, 165
mail, 113

main course, 92
maintenance, 118
marmalade, 85
mat, 55, 60
mattress, 54
mezzanine, 6, 37, 54
mice, 45
minimum wage, 169
minor work, 35
mirror, 53, 55, 60, 66
mortgage, 14, 26, 27, 29, 102
MOT, 136
motor bike, 72
motor vehicles, 136
mountains, 18, 73, 188
mower, 73

nationality, 186
newspapers, 158
New Year, 98, 107
notary, 23, 24, 25, 26, 27, 28, 29, 103
note, 111

occupancy, 106
offer, 24
office, 68
officialdom, 127
orchard, 78
outbuildings, 70

paddling pool, 79
parking, 21, 72
partners, 8
paying, 38, 110
payphone, 66
pension, 8, 134, 135
photographs, 21, 74, 159, 160, 164, 165
pictures, 53
pigeonnier, 20, 33
pillows, 118, 120

Planning Permission, 35
plumber, 118, 171
police,136
pool house, 76
preliminary contract, 27
prices, 104
profit, 5
proprietors, 174
proxy, 28, 29
publicity, 148

qualifications, 4
quotations, 39, 40, 103

radiators, 45
rates, 130, 131
receipt, 109, 110
recommendations, 163
references:
    builders, 38
    staff, 170
regional cooking, 91
renovating, 31, 164
replanning, 33
reservations, 99, 107, 110, 196
restaurants, 16, 20, 88, 104, 144, 196
right of way, 28
roof, 42
rubbish, 81

safety, 77, 194
salad, 90, 92
salt (for pool), 75
sand pit, 79
satellite dish, 65
sea, 17, 187
seminars, 146
septic tank, 27, 47, 81, 124
services, 6, 32
serviettes, 121

sheets, 120
shower, 48, 57, 59, 60
shutters, 44, 118, 121
sideboard, 63, 64, 66
signs, 162, 166
skiing, 15, 18, 168, 190
smoke detector, 62
smoking, 124, 161
social security, 128, 135, 169
Société Civile Immobilière, 27
sofa, 64
solar:
   heating, 45, 76
    shower, 75
soup, 92
squash court, 79
staff, 68, 167
stairs, 44, 68
stationery, 160
sterling, 106, 111, 116, 130
stone, 42
storage, 67
survey, 25, 32
surveyor, 23, 25, 27
swimming pool, 5, 27, 73, 103, 114, 161,
   172, 194
swing, 79

table, 32, 54, 62, 64, 83
table cloths, 121, 126
table d'hôte, 3, 7, 86, 132, 142, 150
table tennis, 66, 79
tax, 26, 27, 78, 104, 115, 128, 131, 135, 141
tea, 56, 100, 190
teenagers, 193
telephone, 29, 56, 68, 111, 115, 116
television, 56, 65, 71, 194
tennis court, 79, 163, 194
terrace, 73
theft, 114

themes, 56
tiles:
   floor, 55, 60, 61
   roof, 42
   wall, 60, 61
timber pests, 44
toddlers, 193
tourist information, 66, 196
tourist office, 17, 126, 151, 163
towels, 121, 122
towns, 20

under blankets, 120

VAT, 38, 132
vegetables, 78, 92
veranda, 32
video, 65
vineyards, 141
visiting card, 160, 162, 165
viticulture, 141
village, 16, 18, 107, 160, 161

wallpaper, 55
walls, 42, 45
wardrobe, 54
washing machine, 46, 68
water, 29, 36, 46, 115, 138
WC, 59, 76
web, 112, 153
weddings, 20, 146, 189
welcome, 126, 190
wild life, 124
windows, 35, 43, 44, 47, 55, 71, 121, 198
wine, 86, 95, 98, 135, 141
woodland, 80
World Heritage Sites, 19
work permit, 2

yoghurt, 80